King Henry the 4th Part 1
By William Shakespeare

Edited by Julien Coallier

Copyright Julien Coallier 2012

All Rights Reserved.

Scenes

Act I – Page 9

Scene 1: London. (The palace)

Scene 2: London. (An apartment of the Prince's)

Scene 3: London. (The palace)

Act II – Page 39

Scene 1: Rochester. (An inn yard)

Scene 2: The road near Gadshill.

Scene 3: Warkworth castle

Scene 4: The Boar's-Head Tavern (Eastcheap)

Act III – Page 93

Scene 1: Bangor. (The Archdeacon's house)

Scene 2: London. (The palace)

Scene 3: Eastcheap. (The Boar's-Head Tavern)

Act IV – Page 127

Scene 1: The rebel camp near Shrewsbury.

Scene 2: A public road near Coventry.

Scene 3: The rebel camp near Shrewsbury.

Scene 4: The Archbishop's palace. (York)

Act V – Page 147

Scene 1: King Henry IV's camp near Shrewsbury.

Scene 2: The rebel camp.

Scene 3: Plain between the camps.

Scene 4: Another part of the field.

Scene 5: Another part of the field.

Characters

Archbishop Scroop (Archbishop of York)

Blunt

Carrier

Chamberlain

Earl of Douglas

Earl of Northumberland

Earl of Westmoreland

Earl of Worcester

Edward Poins

Falstaff (Sir John Falstaff)

First Carrier

First Traveller

Francis (A drawer)

Gadshill

Glendower

Henry IV (King of England)

Prince Henry (Henry V, Harry, King of England)

Hostess Quickly (Hostess of a tavern in Eastcheap)

Henry Percy (Hotspur)

Lady Percy

Lord Bardolph

Messenger

Mortimer (Earl of March)

Ostler

Peto

Prince John (of Lancaster)

Second Carrier

Servant

Sheriff

Sir Michael (A friend to the Archbishop of York)

Thieves

Travellers

Vernon (Of the White Rose, or York, faction)

Vintner

Act I, Scene 1

The palace. (London)

(**King Henry, Lord John** OF **Lancaster**, the **Earl of Westmoreland, Sir Walter Blunt, and others enter**)

Henry IV: So shaken as we are, so wan with care, find we a time for frighted peace to pant and breathe short-winded accents of new broils to be commenced in strands afar remote.

No more the thirsty entrance of this soil shall daub her lips with her own children's blood; nor more shall trenching war channel her fields, nor bruise her flowerets with the armed hoofs of hostile paces.

Those opposed eyes, which, like the meteors of a troubled heaven, all of one nature, of one substance bred, did lately meet in the intestine shock, and furious close of civil butchery.

Shall now, in mutual well-beseeming ranks, march all one way and be no more opposed against acquaintance, kindred and allies.

The edge of war, like an ill-sheathed knife shall no more cut his master, therefore friends, as far as to the sepulchre of Christ whose name we soldier now, under whose blessed cross we are impressed and engaged to fight; forthwith a power of English shall we levy;

Whose arms were moulded in their mothers' womb to chase these pagans in those holy fields, over whose acres walked those blessed feet, which fourteen hundred years ago were nailed for our advantage on the bitter cross.

This our purpose now is twelve month old and bootless, it is to tell you we will go, therefore we meet not now.

Then let me hear of you, my gentle cousin Westmoreland, what yesternight our council did decree in forwarding this dear expedience.

Earl of Westmoreland, my liege, this haste was hot in question, and many limits of the charge set down but yesternight when all athwart there came.

A post from Wales loaden with heavy news, whose worst was, that the noble Mortimer, leading the men of Herefordshire to fight against the irregular and wild Glendower, was by the rude hands of that Welshman taken.

A thousand of his people butchered, upon whose dead corpse there was such misuse, such beastly shameless transformation; by those Welshwomen done as may not be without much shame retold or spoken of.

Henry IV: It seems then that the tidings of this broil brake off our business for the Holy Land, Earl of Westmoreland.

This matched with other, did my gracious lord; for more uneven and unwelcome news came from the north and thus it did import on Holy-good day.

The gallant Hotspur there, young Harry Percy and brave Archibald, that ever-valiant and approved Scot at Holmedon, met where they did spend a sad and bloody houru.

As by discharge of their artillery, and shape of likelihood, the news was told, for he that brought them in the very heat and pride of their contention did take horse; uncertain of the issue any way.

Henry IV: Here is a dear, a true industrious friend; Sir Walter Blunt, new lighted from his horse, stained with the variation of each soil between that Holmedon and this seat of ours.

He hath brought us smooth and welcome news; the Earl of Douglas is discomfited.

Ten thousand bold Scots, two and twenty knights balked in their own blood, did Sir Walter see on Holmedon's plains.

Of prisoners, Hotspur took Mordake the Earl of Fife, and eldest son to beaten Douglas, and the Earl of Athol, of Murray, Angus, and Menteith; and is not this an honourable spoil?

A gallant prize? ha, cousin, is it not?

Earl of Westmoreland, in faith, it is a conquest for a prince to boast of.

Henry IV: Yea, there thou makest me sad and makest me sin in envy that my Lord Northumberland should be the father to so blest a son; a son who is the theme of honour's tongue amongst a grove, the very straightest plant, who is sweet Fortune's minion and her pride.

Whilst I, by looking on the praise of him see riot and dishonour stain the brow of my young Harry.

Oh that it could be proved that some night-tripping fairy had exchanged in cradle-clothes our children where they lay, and called mine Percy, his Plantagenet!

Then would I have his Harry, and he mine, but let him from my thoughts.

What think you, coz, of this young Percy's pride? The prisoners, which he in this adventure hath surprised to his own use; he keeps and sends me word, I shall have none but Mordake Earl of Fife.

Earl of Westmoreland: This is his uncle's teaching, this is Worcester, Malevolent to you in all aspects; which makes him prune himself, and bristle up the crest of youth against your dignity.

Henry IV: But I have sent for him to answer this, and for this cause awhile we must neglect our holy purpose to Jerusalem.

Cousin, on Wednesday next, we our council will hold at Windsor, so inform the lords but come yourself with speed to us again; for more is to be said and to be done than out of anger can be uttered.

Earl of Westmoreland: I will, my liege.

(Exeunt)

Act I, Scene 2

An apartment of the Prince's. (London)

(The Prince of Wales and Falstaff enter)

Falstaff: Now, Hal, what time of day is it, lad?

Prince Henry: Thou art so fat-witted, with drinking of old sack, and unbuttoning thee after supper and sleeping upon benches after noon, thou hast forgotten to demand that truly which thou wouldst truly know.

What a devil hast thou to do with the time of the day? Unless hours were cups of sack and minutes capons and clocks the tongues of bawds and dials the signs of leaping-houses and the blessed sun himself a fair hot wench in flame-coloured taffeta, I see no reason why thou shouldst be so superfluous to demand the time of the day.

Falstaff: Indeed, you come near me now, Hal, for we that take purses go by the moon and the seven stars, and not by Phoebus, he, that wandering knight so fair.

And, I pray to thee, sweet wag, when thou art king, as God save thy grace; majesty I should say, for grace thou wilt have none.

Prince Henry: What, none?

Falstaff: No, by my troth, not so much as will serve to prologue to an egg and butter.

Prince Henry: Well, how then? Come, roundly, roundly.

Falstaff: Merrily then, sweet wag, when thou art king let not us that are squires of the night's body be called thieves of the day's beauty, let us be Diana's foresters, gentlemen of the shade, minions of the moon, and let men say we be men of good government; being governed, as the sea is, by our noble and chaste mistress the moon, under whose countenance we steal.

Prince Henry: Thou sayest well, and it holds well too, for the fortune of us that are the moon's men doth ebb and flow like the sea, being governed, as the sea is, by the moon.

As for proof, now, a purse of gold most resolutely snatched on Monday night and most dissolutely spent on Tuesday morning.

Got with swearing lay by and spent with crying bring in, now in as low an ebb as the foot of the ladder and by and by in as high a flow as the ridge of the gallows.

Falstaff: By the Lord, thou sayest true, lad, and is not my hostess of the tavern a most sweet wench?

Prince Henry: As the honey of Hybla, my old lad of the castle, and is not a buff jerkin a most sweet robe of durance?

Falstaff: How now, how now, mad wag! What, in thy quips and thy quiddities?

What a plague have I to do with a buff jerkin?

Prince Henry: Why, what a pox have I to do with my hostess of the tavern?

Falstaff: Well, thou hast called her to a reckoning many a time and oft.

Prince Henry: Did I ever call for thee to pay thy part?

Falstaff: No, I'll give thee thy due, thou hast paid all there.

Prince Henry: Yea, and elsewhere, so far as my coin would stretch and where it would not, I have used my credit.

Falstaff: Yea, and so used it that were it not here apparent that thou art heir apparent, but I pray to thee sweet wag, shall there be gallows standing in England when thou art king?

Resolution thus fobbed as it is with the rusty curb of old father antic the law?

Do not thou, when thou art king, hang a thief.

Prince Henry: No; thou shalt.

Falstaff: Shall I? Oh rare! By the Lord, I'll be a brave judge.

Prince Henry: Thou judgest false already.

I mean thou shalt have the hanging of the thieves and so become a rare hangman.

Falstaff: Well, Hal, well; and in some sort it jumps with my humour as well as waiting in the court, I can tell you.

Prince Henry: For obtaining of suits?

Falstaff: Yea, for obtaining of suits, whereof the hangman hath no lean wardrobe.

Is blood, I am as melancholy as a gib cat or a lugged bear.

Prince Henry: Or an old lion, or a lover's lute.

Falstaff: Yea, or the drone of a Lincolnshire bagpipe.

Prince Henry: What sayest thou to a hare, or the melancholy of Moor-ditch?

Falstaff: Thou hast the most unsavoury similes and art indeed the most comparative, rascalliest, sweet young prince.

But, Hal, I pray to thee, trouble me no more with vanity.

I would swear to God, thou and I knew where a commodity of good names were to be bought.

An old lord of the council rated me the other day in the street about you, sir, but I marked him not, and yet he talked very wisely but I regarded him not; and yet he talked wisely, and in the street too.

Prince Henry: Thou didst well; for wisdom cries out in the streets, and no man regards it.

Falstaff: Oh thou hast damnable iteration and art indeed able to corrupt a saint.

Thou hast done much harm upon me, Hal; God forgive thee for it! Before I knew thee, Hal, I knew nothing.

Now am I, if a man should speak truly, little better than one of the wicked, I must give over this life and I will give it over by the Lord, and I do not, I am a villain.

I'll be damned for never a king's son in Christendom.

Prince Henry: Where shall we take a purse tomorrow, Jack?

Falstaff: Sounds, where thou wilt, lad, I'll make one; and I do not, call me villain and baffle me.

Prince Henry: I see a good amendment of life in thee; from praying to purse-taking.

Falstaff: Why Hal, it is my vocation Hal; it is no sin for a man to labour in his vocation.

(Enter Poins)

Poins! Now shall we know if Gadshill have set a match.

Oh if men were to be saved by merit, what hole in hell were hot enough for him?

This is the most omnipotent villain that ever cried: Stand to a true man.

Prince Henry: Good morrow, Ned.

Edward Poins: Good morrow, sweet Hal.

What says Monsieur Remorse?

What says Sir John Sack and Sugar? Jack!

How agrees the devil and thee about thy soul that thou soldest him on Good-Friday last for a cup of Madeira, and a cold capon's leg?

Prince Henry: Sir John stands to his word, the devil shall have his bargain, for he was never yet a breaker of proverbs; he will give the devil his due.

Edward Poins: Then art thou damned for keeping thy word with the devil.

Prince Henry: Else he had been damned for cozening the devil.

Edward Poins: But my lads, my lads, to-morrow morning by four o'clock early at Gadshill! There are pilgrims going to Canterbury with rich offerings, and traders riding to London with fat purses.

I have wizards for you all, you have horses for yourselves, Gadshill lies to-night in

Rochester: I have bespoke supper to-morrow night in Eastcheap, we may do it as secure as sleep.

If you will go, I will stuff your purses full of crowns, if you will not, tarry at home and be hanged.

Falstaff: Hear ye, Yedward, if I tarry at home and go not; I'll hang you for going.

Edward Poins: You will, chops?

Falstaff: Hal, wilt thou make one?

Prince Henry: Who, I rob? I a thief? Not I, by my faith.

Falstaff: There's neither honesty, manhood, nor good fellowship in thee, nor thou camest not of the blood royal; if thou darest not stand for ten shillings.

Prince Henry: Well then, once in my days I'll be a madcap.

Falstaff: Why, that's well said.

Prince Henry: Well, come what will, I'll tarry at home.

Falstaff: By the Lord, I'll be a traitor then, when thou art king.

Prince Henry: I care not.

Edward Poins: Sir John, I pray to thee, leave the prince and me alone.

I will lay him down such reasons for this adventure that he shall go.

Falstaff: Well, God give thee the spirit of persuasion and him the ears of profiting, that what thou speakest may move and what he hears may be believed, that the true prince may for recreation sake, prove a false thief; for the poor abuses of the time want countenance.

Farewell.

You shall find me in Eastcheap.

Prince Henry: Farewell, thou latter spring! farewell, All-hallown summer!

(Falstaff exits)

Edward Poins: Now, my good sweet honey lord, ride with us to-morrow.

I have a jest to execute that I cannot manage alone.

Falstaff, Bardolph, Peto and Gadshill shall rob those men that we have already waylaid.

Yourself and I will not be there; and when they have the booty, if you and I do not rob them, cut this head off from my shoulders.

Prince Henry: How shall we part with them in setting forth?

Edward Poins: Why, we will set forth before or after them, and appoint them a place of meeting, wherein it is at our pleasure to fail, and then will they adventure upon the exploit themselves; which they shall have no sooner achieved, but we'll set upon them.

Prince Henry: Yea, but it is like that they will know us by our horses, by our habits and by every other appointment, to be ourselves.

Edward Poins: Tut! Our horses they shall not see, I'll tie them in the wood; our wizards we will change after we leave them.

Sirrah, I have cases of buckram for the nonce to immask our noted outward garments.

Prince Henry: Yea, but I doubt they will be too hard for us.

Edward Poins: Well, for two of them, I know them to be as true-bred cowards as ever turned back; and for the third, if he fight longer than he sees reason, I'll forswear arms.

The virtue of this jest will be the incomprehensible lies that this same fat rogue will tell us when we meet at supper, how thirsty; at least he fought with what wards, what blows, what extremities he endured, and in the reproof of this lies the jest.

Prince Henry: Well, I'll go with thee: provide us all things necessary and meet me to-morrow night in Eastcheap, there I'll sup.

Farewell.

Edward Poins: Farewell, my lord.

(Poins exits)

Henry IV: I know you all, and will awhile uphold the unyoked humour of your idleness, yet herein will I imitate the sun.

Who doth permit the base contagious clouds to smother up his beauty from the world, that, when he please again to be himself, being wanted he may be more wondered at by breaking through the foul and ugly mists of vapours that did seem to strangle him.

If all the year were playing holidays, to sport would be as tedious as to work, but when they seldom come, they wished for come, and nothing pleaseth but rare accidents.

So when this loose behavior I throw off and pay the debt I never promised, by how much better than my word I am, by so much shall I falsify men's hopes.

And like bright metal on a sullen ground, my reformation, glittering over my fault, shall show more goodly and attract more eyes than that which hath no foil to set it off.

I'll so offend to make offence a skill, redeeming time when men think least I will.

(Exits)

Act I, Scene 3

The palace. (London)

(The King, Northumberland, Worcester, Hotspur, Sir Walter Blunt, with others enter)

Henry IV: My blood hath been too cold and temperate; unapt to stir at these indignities, and you have found me; for accordingly you tread upon my patience.

Be sure I will from henceforth rather be myself, mighty and to be feared than my condition, which hath been smooth as oil, soft as young down, and therefore lost that title of respect; which the proud soul ne'er pays but to the proud.

Earl of Worcester: Our house, my sovereign liege, little deserves the scourge of greatness to be used on it; and that same greatness too which our own hands have help to make so portly.

Earl of Northumberland: My lord.

Henry IV: Worcester, get thee gone for I do see danger and disobedience in thine eye.

Oh sir, your presence is too bold and peremptory, majesty, which might never yet endure the moody frontier of a servant brow.

You have good leave to leave us: when we need your use and counsel, we shall send for you.

(Worcester exits)

You were about to speak.

(To North)

Earl of Northumberland: Yea, my good lord.

Those prisoners in your highness' name demanded, which Harry Percy here at Holmedon took; were as he says, not with such strength denied as is delivered to your majesty.

Either envy, therefore, or misprison is guilty of this fault and not my son.

Hotspur (Henry Percy): My liege, I did deny no prisoners.

I remember when the fight was done, when I was dry with rage and extreme toil; breathless and faint, leaning upon my sword, came there a certain lord, neat, and trimly dressed, fresh as a bridegroom.

His chin new reaped, showed like a stubble-land at harvest-home; he was perfumed like a milliner and it twist his finger and his thumb; he held a pouncet-box, which ever and anon.

He gave his nose and took it away again, who therewith angry when it next came there, took it in snuff; and still he smiled and talked, and as the soldiers bore dead bodies by.

He called them untaught knaves, unmannerly to bring a slovenly unhandsome corpse between the wind and his nobility.

With many holiday and lady terms he questioned me, amongst the rest he demanded my prisoners in your majesty's behalf.

I then, all smarting with my wounds being cold to be so pestered with a popinjay, out of my grief and my impatience answered neglectingly.

I know not what he should or he should not, for he made me mad to see him shine so brisk and smell so sweet, and talk so like a waiting-gentlewoman of guns and drums and wounds, God save the mark!

And telling me the sovereign'st thing on earth was parmaceti for an inward bruise, and that it was great pity; so it was this villainous salt-petre should be digged, put of the bowels of the harmless earth; which many a good tall fellow had destroyed so cowardly, but for these vile guns he would himself have been a soldier.

This bald unjointed chat of his, my lord, I answered indirectly, as I said; and I beseech you, let not his report come current for an accusation between my love and your high majesty.

Blunt: The circumstance considered, good my lord, whatever Lord Harry Percy then had said to such a person and in such a place, at such a time with all the rest retold; may reasonably die and never rise to do him wrong or any way impeach what then he said, so he unsay it now.

Henry IV: Why, yet he doth deny his prisoners, but with proviso and exception, that we at our own charge shall ransom straight his brother-in-law, the foolish Mortimer; who on my soul, hath wilfully betrayed the lives of those that he did lead to fight against that great magician.

Damned Glendower, whose daughter, as we hear, the Earl of March hath lately married.

Shall our coffers, then, be emptied to redeem a traitor home?

Shall we but treason? And indent with fears when they have lost and forfeited themselves?

No, on the barren mountains let him starve, for I shall never hold that man my friend whose tongue shall ask me for one penny cost to ransom home revolted Mortimer.

Hotspur (Henry Percy): Revolted Mortimer!

He never did fall off, my sovereign liege, but by the chance of war to prove that true needs no more but one tongue for all those wounds, those mouthed wounds, which valiantly he took when on the gentle Severn's sedgy bank.

In single opposition, hand to hand, he did confound the best part of an hour in changing hardiment with great Glendower.

Three times they breathed and three times did they drink upon agreement, of swift Severn's fled, who then, affrighted with their bloody looks, ran fearfully among the trembling reeds; and hid his crisp head in the hollow bank, bloodstained with these valiant combatants.

Never did base and rotten policy colour her working with such deadly wounds, nor could the noble Mortimer receive so many, and all willingly.

Then let not him be slandered with revolt.

Henry IV: Thou dost belie him, Percy, thou dost belie him, he never did encounter with

Glendower: I tell thee, he durst as well have met the devil alone as owen Glendower for an enemy.

Art thou not ashamed? But sirrah, henceforth let me not hear you speak of Mortimer.

Send me your prisoners with the speediest means, or you shall hear in such a kind from me as will displease you.

My Lord Northumberland, we licence your departure with your son.

Send us your prisoners, or you will hear of it.

(Exeunt King Henry, Blunt, and entourage)

Hotspur (Henry Percy): And if the devil come and roar for them, I will not send them.

I will after straight, and tell him so, for I will ease my heart; Albeit I make a hazard of my head.

Earl of Northumberland: What, drunk with choler? stay and pause awhile.

Here comes your uncle.

(Worcester re-enters)

Hotspur (Henry Percy): Speak of Mortimer!

I will speak of him, and let my soul want mercy, if I do not join with him.

Yea, on his part I'll empty all these veins, and shed my dear blood drop by drop in the dust, but I will lift the down-trod Mortimer as high in the air as this unthankful king, Aas this ingrate and cankered Bolingbroke.

Earl of Northumberland: Brother, the king hath made your nephew mad.

Earl of Worcester: Who struck this heat up after I was gone?

Hotspur (Henry Percy): He will forsooth, have all my prisoners, and when I urged the ransom once again of my wife's brother, then his cheek looked pale, and on my face he turned an eye of death; trembling even at the name of Mortimer.

Earl of Worcester: I cannot blame him: was not he proclaimed by Richard that dead is the next of blood?

Earl of Northumberland: He was; I heard the proclamation, and then it was when the unhappy king; whose wrongs in us God pardon! Did set forth upon his Irish expedition from whence he intercepted did return to be deposed and shortly murdered.

Earl of Worcester: And for whose death we in the world's wide mouth live scandalized and foully spoken of.

Hotspur (Henry Percy): But soft, I pray you; did King Richard then proclaim my brother Edmund Mortimer heir to the crown?

Earl of Northumberland: He did, myself did hear it.

Hotspur (Henry Percy): Nay, then I cannot blame his cousin king, that wished him on the barren mountains starve.

But shall it be that you, that set the crown upon the head of this forgetful man and for his sake wear the detested blot of murderous subornation, shall it be, that you a world of curses undergo; being the agents, or base second means, the cords, the ladder, or the hangman rather?

Oh pardon me that I descend so low, to show the line and the predicament wherein you range under this subtle king; shall it for shame be spoken in these days, or fill up chronicles in time to come.

That men of your nobility and power did gage them both in an unjust behalf, as both of you, God pardon it! Have done to put down Richard, that sweet lovely rose, and plant this thorn, this canker, Bolingbroke?

Shall it in more shame be further spoken, that you are fooled, discarded and shook off by him for whom these shames ye underwent?

No, yet time serves wherein you may redeem your banished honours and restore yourselves into the good thoughts of the world again, revenge the jeering and disdained contempt of this proud king who studies day and night to answer all the debt he owes to you; even with the bloody payment of your deaths, therefore I say…

Earl of Worcester: Peace cousin, say no more, and now I will unclasp a secret book, and to your quick-conceiving discontents I'll read you matter deep and dangerous as full of peril and adventurous spirit, as to over-walk a current roaring loud on the unsteadfast footing of a spear.

Hotspur (Henry Percy): If he fall in, good night! or sink or swim.

Send danger from the east unto the west, so honour cross it from the north to south, and let them grapple.

Oh the blood more stirs to rouse a lion than to start a hare!

Earl of Northumberland: Imagination of some great exploit drives him beyond the bounds of patience.

Hotspur (Henry Percy): By heaven, methinks it were an easy leap, to pluck bright honour from the pale-faced moon, or dive into the bottom of the deep where fathom-line could never touch the ground.

Pluck up drowned honour by the locks, so he that doth redeem her thence might wear without corrival, all her dignities out upon this half-faced fellowship!

Earl of Worcester: He apprehends a world of figures here, but not the form of what he should attend.

Good cousin, give me audience for a while.

Hotspur (Henry Percy): I cry you mercy.

Earl of Worcester: Those same noble Scots that are your prisoners.

Hotspur (Henry Percy): I'll keep them all, by God, he shall not have a Scot of them.

No, if a Scot would save his soul, he shall not; I'll keep them, by this hand.

Earl of Worcester: You start away and lend no ear unto my purposes.

Those prisoners you shall keep.

Hotspur (Henry Percy): Nay, I will, that's flat.

He said he would not ransom Mortimer and forbad my tongue to speak of Mortimer;but I will find him when he lies asleep, and in his ear I'll holla 'Mortimer!'

Nay, I'll have a starling shall be taught to speak nothing but Mortimer, and give it him to keep his anger still in motion.

Earl of Worcester: Hear you, cousin, a word.

Hotspur (Henry Percy): All studies here I solemnly defy, save how to gall and pinch this Bolingbroke.

That same sword-and-buckler Prince of Wales, but that I think his father loves him not and would be glad he met with some mischance; I would have him poisoned with a pot of ale.

Earl of Worcester: Farewell, kinsman: I'll talk to you when you are better tempered to attend.

Earl of Northumberland: Why, what a wasp-stung and impatient fool art thou to break into this woman's mood, tying thine ear to no tongue but thine own!

Hotspur (Henry Percy): Why, look you, I am whipped and scourged with rods, nettled and stung with pismires, when I hear of this vile politician, Bolingbroke.

In Richard's time, what do you call the place?

A plague upon it, it is in Gloucestershire; it was where the madcap duke his uncle kept his uncle York, where I first bowed my knee unto this king of smiles, this Bolingbroke, is blood! When you and he came back from Ravenspurgh.

Earl of Northumberland: At Berkley castle.

Hotspur (Henry Percy): You say true; why, what a candy deal of courtesy this fawning greyhound then did proffer me!

Look, when his infant fortune came to age, and a gentle Harry Percy, and kind cousin;

Oh the devil take such cozeners!

God forgive me! Good uncle tell your tale, I have done.

Earl of Worcester: Nay, if you have not, to it again; we will stay your leisure.

Hotspur (Henry Percy): I have done, in faith.

Earl of Worcester: Then once more to your Scottish prisoners.

Deliver them up without their ransom straight and make the Douglas' son your only means for powers in Scotland, which for divers reasons which I shall send you written; be assured you, my lord will easily be granted.

(To Northumberland)

Your son in Scotland being thus employed, shall secretly into the bosom creep of that same noble prelate, well-beloved the archbishop.

Hotspur (Henry Percy): Of York, is it not?

Earl of Worcester: True; who bears hard his brother's death at Bristol, the Lord Scroop.

I speak not this in estimation, as what I think might be, but what I know is ruminated, plotted and set down, and only stays but to behold the face of that occasion that shall bring it on.

Hotspur (Henry Percy): I smell it: upon my life, it will do well.

Earl of Northumberland: Before the game is afoot, thou still let'st slip.

Hotspur (Henry Percy): Why, it cannot choose but be a noble plot, and then the power of Scotland and of York to join with Mortimer, ha?

Earl of Worcester: And so they shall.

Hotspur (Henry Percy): In faith, it is exceedingly well aimed.

Earl of Worcester: And it is no little reason bids us speed to save our heads by raising of a head; for bear ourselves as even as we can the king will always think him in our debt, and think we think ourselves unsatisfied till he hath found a time to pay us home.

See already how he doth begin to make us strangers to his looks of love.

Hotspur (Henry Percy): He does, he does, we'll be revenged on him.

Earl of Worcester: Cousin, farewell: no further go in this than I by letters shall direct your course.

When time is ripe, which will be suddenly, I'll steal to Glendower and Lord Mortimer; where you and Douglas and our powers at once as I will fashion it, shall happily meet to bear our fortunes in our own strong arms, which now we hold at much uncertainty.

Earl of Northumberland: Farewell, good brother.

We shall thrive, I trust.

Hotspur (Henry Percy): Uncle, Adieu.

Oh let the hours be short till fields and blows and groans applaud our sport!

(Exeunt)

Act II, Scene 1

An inn yard. (Rochester)

(A Carrier with a lantern in his hand enters)

First Carrier: Heigh-oh! And it be not four by the day, I'll be hanged.

Charles' wain is over the new chimney, and yet our horse not packed.

What, ostler!

Ostler: (Within area) Ah no, ah no.

First Carrier: I pray to thee, Tom, beat Cut's saddle, put a few flocks in the point, poor jade, is wrung in the withers out of all cess.

(Another Carrier enters)

Second Carrier: Peas and beans are as dank here as a dog, and that is the next way to give poor jades the bots.

This house is turned upside down since Robin Ostler died.

First Carrier: Poor fellow, never joyed since the price of oats rose; it was the death of him.

Second Carrier: I think this be the most villainous house in all London road for fleas.

I am stung like a tench.

First Carrier: Like a tench! By the mass, there is never a king christen could be better bit than I have been since the first cock.

Second Carrier: Why, they will allow us never a jordan, and then we leak in your chimney, and your chamber-lie breeds fleas like a loach.

First Carrier: What, ostler! come away and be hanged!

Second Carrier: I have a gammon of bacon and two razors of ginger to be delivered as far as Charing-cross.

First Carrier: God's body! the turkeys in my pannier are quite starved.

What, ostler! A plague on thee! Hast thou never an eye in thy head? Canst not hear?

And were it not as good deed as drink, to break the pate on thee, I am a very villain.

Come, and be hanged! Hast thou no faith in thee?

(Gadshill enters)

Gadshill: Good morrow, carriers.

What's o'clock?

First Carrier: I think it be two o'clock.

Gadshill: I pray thee lend me thy lantern, to see my gelding in the stable.

First Carrier: Nay, by God, soft; I know a trick worth two of that, in faith.

Gadshill: I pray thee, lend me thine.

Second Carrier: Ay, when? Can'st tell? Lend me thy lantern quoth he merrily, I'll see thee hanged first.

Gadshill: Sirrah carrier, what time do you mean to come to London?

Second Carrier: Time enough to go to bed with a candle, I warrant thee.

Come, neighbour Mugs, we'll call up the gentleman; they will along with company, for they have great charge.

(Exeunt carriers)

Gadshill: What, oh! chamberlain!

Chamberlain: (Within area) At hand, quoth pick-purse.

Gadshill: That's even as fair as, at hand, quoth the chamberlain; for thou variest no more from picking of purses than giving direction doth from labouring, thou layest the plot how.

(Chamberlain enters)

Chamberlain: Good morrow, Master Gadshill.

It holds current that I told you yesternight.

There's a franklin in the wild of Kent hath brought three hundred marks with him in gold.

I heard him tell it to one of his company last night at supper, a kind of auditor, one that hath abundance of charge too, God knows what.

They are up already, and call for eggs and butter, they will away presently.

Gadshill: Sirrah, if they meet not with Saint Nicholas' clerks, I'll give thee this neck.

Chamberlain: No, I'll none of it: I pray thee keep that for the hangman; for I know thou worshippest St. Nicholas as truly as a man of falsehood may.

Gadshill: What talkest thou to me of the hangman? If I hang I'll make a fat pair of gallows; for if I hang old Sir John hangs with me, and thou knowest he is no starveling.

Tut! There are other Trojans that thou dreamest not of, the which for sport sake are content to do the profession some grace; that would if matters should be looked into for their own credit sake and make all whole.

I am joined with no foot-land rakers, no long-staff sixpenny strikers, none of these mad mustachio purple-hued malt-worms; but with nobility and tranquillity, burgomasters and great oneyers, such as can hold in, such as will strike sooner than speak, and speak sooner than drink, and drink sooner than pray.

And yet, sounds, I lie, for they pray continually to their saint, the commonwealth; or rather, not pray to her, but prey on her, for they ride up and down on her and make her their boots.

Chamberlain: What, the commonwealth their boots? Will she hold out water in foul way?

Gadshill: She will, she will; justice hath liquored her.

We steal as in a castle, cocksure, we have the receipt of fern-seed, we walk invisible.

Chamberlain: Nay, by my faith, I think you are more beholding to the night than to fern-seed for your walking invisible.

Gadshill: Give me thy hand: thou shalt have a share in our purchase, as I am a true man.

Chamberlain: Nay, rather let me have it, as you are a false thief.

Gadshill: Go to, homo is a common name to all men.

Bid the ostler bring my gelding out of the stable.

Farewell, you muddy knave.

(Exeunt)

Act II, Scene 2

The highway, near Gadshill.

(Prince Henry and Poins enter)

Edward Poins: Come, shelter, shelter: I have removed Falstaff's horse, and he frets like a gummed velvet.

Prince Henry: Stand close.

(Falstaff enters)

Falstaff: Poins! Poins, and be hanged! Poins!

Prince Henry: Peace, ye fat-kidneyed rascal! What a brawling dost thou keep!

Falstaff: Where's Poins, Hal?

Prince Henry: He is walked up to the top of the hill, I'll go seek him.

Falstaff: I am accursed to rob in that thief's company, the rascal hath removed my horse, and tied him I know not where.

If I travel but four foot by the squier further afoot, I shall break my wind.

Well, I doubt not but to die a fair death for all this, if I escape hanging for killing that rogue.

I have forsworn his company hourly any time this two and twenty years, and yet I am bewitched with the rogue's company.

If the rascal hath not given me medicines to make me love him, I'll be hanged; it could not be else.

I have drunk medicines Poins!

Hal! a plague upon you both! Bardolph! Peto!

I'll starve here I'll rob a foot further, and it were not as good a deed as drink, to turn true man and to leave these rogues, I am the veriest varlet that ever chewed with a tooth.

Eight yards of uneven ground is threescore and ten miles afoot with me, and the stony-hearted villains know it well enough.

A plague upon it when thieves cannot be true one to another!

(They whistle)

Whew! A plague upon you all! Give me my horse you rogues, give me my horse and be hanged!

Prince Henry: Peace, ye fat-guts! Lie down, lay thine ear close to the ground and list if thou canst hear the tread of travellers.

Falstaff: Have you any levers to lift me up again, being down? Is blood, I'll not bear mine own flesh so far afoot again for all the coin in thy father's exchequer.

What a plague mean ye to colt me thus?

Prince Henry: Thou liest; thou art not colted, thou art uncolted.

Falstaff: I pray to thee, good Prince Hal, help me to my horse, good king's son.

Prince Henry: Out, ye rogue! Shall I be your ostler?

Falstaff: Go, hang thyself in thine own heir-apparent garters! If I be taken, I'll peach for this.

And I have not ballads made on you all and sung to filthy tunes, let a cup of sack be my poison, when a jest is so forward and afoot too, I hate it!

(Gadshill, Bardolph and Peto enter)

Gadshill: Stand.

Falstaff: So I do, against my will.

Edward Poins: Oh it is our setter, I know his voice.

Bardolph, what news? Honey of the king's coming down the hill, it is going to the king's exchequer.

Falstaff: You lie, ye rogue, it is going to the king's tavern.

Gadshill: There's enough to make us all.

Falstaff: To be hanged.

Prince Henry: Sirs, you four shall front them in the narrow lane; Ned, Poins, and I will walk lower.

If they escape from your encounter, then they light on us.

Peto: How many be there of them?

Gadshill: Some eight or ten.

Falstaff: Will they not rob us?

Prince Henry: What, a coward, Sir John Paunch?

Falstaff: Indeed, I am not John of Gaunt, your grandfather, but yet no coward, Hal.

Prince Henry: Well, we leave that to the proof.

Edward Poins: Sirrah Jack, thy horse stands behind the hedge when thou needest him, there thou shalt find him.

Farewell, and stand fast.

Falstaff: Now cannot I strike him, if I should be hanged.

Prince Henry: Ned, where are our disguises?

Edward Poins: Here, hard by, stand close.

(Exeunt Prince Henry and Poins)

Falstaff: Now, my masters, happy man be his dole, say I, every man to his business.

(The Travellers enter)

First Carrier: Come, neighbour: the boy shall lead our horses down the hill, we'll walk afoot awhile, and ease our legs.

Thieves: Stand!

Travellers: Jesus bless us!

Falstaff: Strike; down with them; cut the villains' throats.

Ah! whoreson caterpillars! Bacon-fed knaves!

They hate us youth, down with them, fleece them.

Travellers: Oh we are undone, both we and ours for ever!

Falstaff: Hang ye, gorbellied knaves, are ye undone? No, ye fat chuffs.

I would your store were here! On, bacons, on!

What, ye knaves! young men must live.

You are Grand-jurors, are ye? We'll jure ye, in faith.

(Here they rob them and bind them. Exeunt)

(Prince Henry and Poins re-enter)

Prince Henry: The thieves have bound the true men.

Now could thou and I rob the thieves and go merrily to London, it would be argument for a week, laughter for a month and a good jest for ever.

Edward Poins: Stand close, I hear them coming.

(The Thieves enter again)

Falstaff: Come, my masters, let us share, and then to horse before day.

An the Prince and Poins be not two arrant cowards, there's no equity stirring.

There's no more valour in that Poins than in a wild-duck.

Prince Henry: Your money!

Edward Poins: Villains!

(As they are sharing, the Prince and Poins set upon them, they all run away)

(Falstaff, after a blow or two, runs away too, leaving the booty behind them)

Prince Henry: Got with much ease.

Now merrily to horse, the thieves are all scattered and possessed with fear so strongly that they dare not meet each other; each takes his fellow for an officer.

Away, good Ned.

Falstaff sweats to death, and lards the lean earth as he walks along.

Were 't not for laughing, I should pity him.

Edward Poins: How the rogue roared!

(Exeunt)

Act II, Scene 3

Warkworth castle

(Hotspur enters solus, reading a letter)

Hotspur (Henry Percy): But for mine own part, my lord, I could be well contented to be there in respect of the love I bear your house.

He could be contented, why is he not then?

In respect of the love he bears our house, he shows in this, he loves his own barn better than he loves our house.

Let me see some more, the purpose you undertake is dangerous, why that's certain.

It is dangerous to take a cold, to sleep, to drink; but I tell you my lord fool, out of this nettle, danger, we pluck this flower, safety.

The purpose you undertake is dangerous; the friends you have named uncertain, the time itself unsorted, and your whole plot too light for the counterpoise of so great an opposition.

Say you so, say you so? I say unto you again, you are a shallow cowardly hind, and you lie.

What a lack-brain is this! By the Lord, our plot is a good plot as ever was laid; our friends true and constant.

A good plot, good friends, and full of expectation, an excellent plot, very good friends.

What a frosty-spirited rogue is this! Why, my lord of York commends the plot and the

general course of action.

And I were now by this rascal, I could brain him with his lady's fan.

Is there not my father, my uncle and myself? lord Edmund Mortimer, My lord of York and Owen Glendower? Is there not besides the Douglas?

Have I not all their letters to meet me in arms by the ninth of the next month? And are they not some of them set forward already?

What a pagan rascal is this! An infidel! Ha! You shall see now in very sincerity of fear and cold heart, will he to the king and lay open all our proceedings.

Oh I could divide myself and go to buffets, for moving such a dish of skim milk with so honourable an action! Hang him! Let him tell the king: we are prepared.

I will set forward to-night.

(Lady Percy enters)

How now, Kate! I must leave you within these two hours.

Lady Percy: Oh my good lord, why are you thus alone?

For what offence have I this fortnight been a banished woman from my Harry's bed?

Tell me, sweet lord, what is it that takes from thee thy stomach, pleasure and thy golden sleep?

Why dost thou bend thine eyes upon the earth, and start so often when thou sit'st alone?

Why hast thou lost the fresh blood in thy cheeks, and given my treasures and my rights of thee to thick-eyed musing and cursed melancholy?

In thy faint slumbers I by thee have watched, and heard thee murmur tales of iron wars; speak terms of manage to thy bounding steed, cry: Courage! To the field!

Thou hast talked Of sallies and retires, of trenches, tents, of palisadoes, frontiers, parapets, of basilisks, of cannon, culverin, of prisoners' ransom and of soldiers slain, and all the currents of a heady fight.

Thy spirit within thee hath been so at war, and thus hath so bestirred thee in thy sleep, that beads of sweat have stood upon thy brow like bubbles in a late-disturbed stream; and in thy face strange motions have appeared, such as we see when men restrain their breath on some great sudden hest.

Oh what portents are these? Some heavy business hath my lord in hand, and I must know it, else he loves me not.

Hotspur (Henry Percy): What, oh!

(Servant enters)

Is Gilliams with the packet gone?

Servant: He is, my lord, an hour ago.

Hotspur (Henry Percy): Hath Butler brought those horses from the sheriff?

Servant: One horse, my lord, he brought even now.

Hotspur (Henry Percy): What horse? A roan, a crop-ear, is it not?

Servant: It is, my lord.

Hotspur (Henry Percy): That roan shall by my throne.

Well, I will back him straight; oh hope! Bid Butler lead him forth into the park.

(Servant exits)

Lady Percy: But hear you, my lord.

Hotspur (Henry Percy): What say'st thou, my lady?

Lady Percy: What is it carries you away?

Hotspur (Henry Percy): Why, my horse, my love, my horse.

Lady Percy: Out, you mad-headed ape!

A weasel hath not such a deal of spleen as you are tossed with.

In faith I'll know your business Harry, that I will.

I fear my brother Mortimer doth stir about his title, and hath sent for you to line his enterprise; but if you go.

Hotspur (Henry Percy): So far afoot, I shall be weary, love.

Lady Percy: Come, come, you paraquito, answer me directly unto this question that I ask.

In faith, I'll break thy little finger, Harry; and if thou wilt not tell me all things true.

Hotspur (Henry Percy): Away,

Away, you trifler! Love! I love thee not, I care not for thee, Kate.

This is no world to play with mammets and to tilt with lips.

We must have bloody noses and cracked crowns, and pass them current too.

God's me, my horse!

What say'st thou, Kate? What would'st thou have with me?

Lady Percy: Do you not love me? Do you not, indeed?

Well do not then, for since you love me not, I will not love myself.

Do you not love me? Nay, tell me if you speak in jest or no.

Hotspur (Henry Percy): Come, wilt thou see me ride?

And when I am on horseback, I will swear I love thee infinitely, but hark you, Kate; I must not have you henceforth question me whither I go, nor reason whereabout.

Whither I must, I must; and, to conclude, this evening must I leave you, gentle Kate.

I know you wise, but yet no farther wise than Harry Percy's wife.

Constant you are, but yet a woman, and for secrecy no lady closer, for I well believe thou wilt not utter what thou dost not know; and so far will I trust thee, gentle Kate.

Lady Percy: How! So far?

Hotspur (Henry Percy): Not an inch further, but hark you, Kate.

Whither I go, thither shall you go too; to-day will I set forth, to-morrow you.

Will this content you, Kate?

Lady Percy: It must of force.

(Exeunt)

Act II, Scene 4

The Boar's-Head Tavern (Eastcheap)

(Prince Henry and Poins enter)

Prince Henry: Ned, pray to thee, come out of that fat room, and lend me thy hand to laugh a little.

Edward Poins: Where hast been, Hal?

Prince Henry: With three or four loggerheads amongst three or four score hogsheads.

I have sounded the very base-string of humility.

Sirrah, I am sworn brother to a leash of drawers; and can call them all by their christen names, as Tom, Dick, and First Carrier.

They take it already upon their salvation, that though I be but the prince of Wales, yet I am king of courtesy; and tell me flatly I am no proud Jack, like Falstaff, but a Corinthian, a lad of mettle, a good boy by the Lord, so they call me; and when I am king of England, I shall command all the good lads in Eastcheap.

They call drinking deep, dyeing scarlet. and when you breathe in your watering, they cry: hem! and bid you play it off.

To conclude, I am so good a proficient in one quarter of an hour, that I can drink with any tinker in his own language during my life.

I tell thee, Ned, thou hast lost much honour, that thou wert not with me in this sweet action, but sweet Ned, to sweeten which name of Ned I give thee this pennyworth of sugar.

Clapped even now into my hand by an under-skinker, one that never spake other English in his life than eight shillings and sixpence' and you are welcome, with this shrill addition: Ah no, ah no sir! Score a pint of bastard in the Half-Moon, or so, but Ned to drive away the time till Falstaff come, I pray to thee, do thou stand in some by-room, while I question my puny drawer to what end he gave me the sugar; and do thou never leave calling Francis, that his tale to me may be nothing but Ah no.

Step aside and I'll show thee a precedent.

Edward Poins: Francis!

Prince Henry: Thou art perfect.

Edward Poins: Francis!

(Exit Poins)

(Francis enter)

First Carrier: Ah no, ah no, sir.

Look down into the Pomgarnet, Ralph.

Prince Henry: Come hither, First Carrier.

First Carrier: My lord?

Prince Henry: How long hast thou to serve, Francis?

First Carrier: Forsooth, five years, and as much as to…

Edward Poins: (Within Area) Francis!

First Carrier: Ah no, ah no sir.

Prince Henry: Five year! by'r lady, a long lease for the clinking of pewter, but, Francis, darest thou be so valiant as to play the coward with thy indenture and show it a fair pair of heels and run from it?

First Carrier: Oh Lord, sir, I'll be sworn upon all the books in England, I could find in my heart.

Edward Poins: (Within Area) Francis!

First Carrier: Ah no sir.

Prince Henry: How old art thou, Francis?

First Carrier: Let me see, about Michaelmas next I shall be.

Edward Poins: **(Within Area)** Francis!

First Carrier: Ah no sir.

Pray stay a little, my lord.

Prince Henry: Nay, but hark you.

Francis: for the sugar thou gavest me,I twas a pennyworth, wast it not?

First Carrier: Oh Lord, I would it had been two!

Prince Henry: I will give thee for it a thousand pound, ask me when thou wilt, and thou shalt have it.

Edward Poins: (Within area) Francis!

First Carrier: Ah no, ah no.

Henry IV: Ah no, Francis? No Francis, but to-morrow Francis, or Francis of Thursday, or indeed Francis when thou wilt; but Francis!

First Carrier: My lord?

Prince Henry: Wilt thou rob this leathern jerkin, crystal-button, not-pated, agate-ring, puke-stocking, caddis-garter, smooth-tongue, Spanish-pouch…

First Carrier: Oh Lord, sir, who do you mean?

Prince Henry: Why, then, your brown bastard is your only drink for look you, Francis, your white canvas doublet will sully.

In Barbary sir, it cannot come to so much.

First Carrier: What, sir?

Edward Poins: (Within area) Francis!

Prince Henry: Away, you rogue! Dost thou not hear them call?

(Here they both call him; the drawer stands amazed, not knowing which way to go)

(Vintner enters)

Vintner: What, standest thou still, and hearest such a calling? Look to the guests within.

(Francis exits)

My lord, old Sir John, with half-a-dozen more are at the door, shall I let them in?

Prince Henry: Let them alone awhile, and then open the door.

(Vintner Exits)

Poins!

(Poins re-enters)

Edward Poins: Ah no, ah no sir.

Prince Henry: Sirrah, Falstaff and the rest of the thieves are at the door.

Shall we be merry?

Edward Poins: As merry as crickets, my lad.

But hark ye, what cunning match have you made with this jest of the drawer? Come, what's the issue?

Prince Henry: I am now of all humours that have showed themselves humours since the old days of goodman Adam to the pupil age of this present twelve o'clock at midnight.

(Francis re-enters)

What's o'clock, Francis?

First Carrier: Ah no, ah no sir.

(Exits)

Prince Henry: That ever this fellow should have fewer words than a parrot, and yet the son of a woman!

His industry is upstairs and downstairs, his eloquence the parcel of a reckoning.

I am not yet of Percy's mind, the Hotspur of the north, he that kills me some six or seven dozen of Scots at a breakfast, washes his hands, and says to his wife: Fie upon this quiet life! I want work.

Oh my sweet Harry, says she, how many hast thou killed to-day?

Give my roan horse a drench, says he; and answers: Some fourteen an hour after: a trifle, a trifle.

I pray to thee, call in Falstaff.

I'll play Percy, and that damned brawn shall play Dame Mortimer his wife.

Rivo! says the drunkard.

Call in ribs, call in tallow.

(Falstaff, Gadshill, Bardolph, and Peto enter, Francis following with wine)

Edward Poins: Welcome, Jack: where hast thou been?

Falstaff: A plague of all cowards, I say, and a vengeance too!

Merrily and amen! Give me a cup of sack boy.

Here I lead this life long, I'll sew nether stocks and mend them and foot them too.

A plague of all cowards!

Give me a cup of sack, rogue.

Is there no virtue extant?

(He drinks)

Prince Henry: Didst thou never see Titan kiss a dish of butter?

Pitiful-hearted Titan, that melted at the sweet tale of the sun's! If thou didst, then behold that compound.

Falstaff: You rogue, here's lime in this sack too, there is nothing but roguery to be found in villainous man.

Yet a coward is worse than a cup of sack with lime in it.

A villainous coward! Go thy ways, old Jack, die when thou wilt; if manhood, good manhood, be not forgot upon the face of the earth, then am I a shotten herring.

There live not three good men unhanged in England, and one of them is fat and grows old.

God help the while! A bad world, I say.

I would if I were a weaver; I could sing psalms or anything.

A plague of all cowards, I say still.

Prince Henry: How now, wool-sack! What mutter you?

Falstaff: A king's son! If I do not beat thee out of thy

kingdom with a dagger of lath, and drive all thy subjects afore thee like a flock of wild-geese, I'll never wear hair on my face more.

You Prince of Wales!

Prince Henry: Why, you whoreson round man, what's the matter?

Falstaff: Are not you a coward? Answer me to that, and Poins there?

Edward Poins: Ye fat paunch, an ye call me coward, by the Lord, I'll stab thee.

Falstaff: I call thee coward! I'll see thee damned were I call thee coward, but I would give a thousand pound if I could run as fast as thou canst.

You are straight enough in the shoulders, you care not who sees your back.

Call you that backing of your friends? A plague upon such backing!

Give me them that will face me.

Give me a cup of sack, I am a rogue, if I drunk to-day.

Prince Henry: Oh villain! Thy lips are scarce wiped since thou drunkest last.

Falstaff: All's one for that.

(He drinks)

A plague of all cowards, still say I.

Prince Henry: What's the matter?

Falstaff: What's the matter! There be four of us here have taken a thousand pound this day morning.

Prince Henry: Where is it, Jack? Where is it?

Falstaff: Where is it! Taken from us it is: a hundred upon poor four of us.

Prince Henry: What, a hundred, man?

Falstaff: I am a rogue, if I were not at half-sword with a dozen of them two hours together.

I have escaped by miracle.

I am eight times thrust through the doublet, four through the hose, my buckler cut through and through, my sword hacked like a handsaw; ecce signum!

I never dealt better since I was a man, all would not do.

A plague of all cowards! Let them speak, if they speak more or less than truth, they are villains and the sons of darkness.

Prince Henry: Speak, sirs; how was it?

Gadshill: We four set upon some dozen—

Falstaff: Sixteen at least, my lord.

Gadshill: And bound them.

Peto: No, no, they were not bound.

Falstaff: You rogue, they were bound, every man of them, or I am a Jew else, a Hebrew Jew.

Gadshill: As we were sharing, some six or seven fresh men set upon us…

Falstaff: And unbound the rest, and then come in the other.

Prince Henry: What, fought you with them all?

Falstaff: All! I know not what you call all; but if I fought not with fifty of them, I am a bunch of radish.

If there were not two or three and fifty upon poor old Jack, then am I no two-legged creature.

Prince Henry: Pray God you have not murdered some of them.

Falstaff: Nay, that's past praying for.

I have peppered two of them, two I am sure I have paid, two rogues in buckram suits.

I tell thee what, Hal, if I tell thee a lie spit in my face, call me horse.

Thou knowest my old ward, here I lay and thus I bore my point.

Four rogues in buckram let drive at me…

Prince Henry: What, four? Thou saidst but two even now.

Falstaff: Four, Hal, I told thee four.

Edward Poins: Ay, ay, he said four.

Falstaff: These four came all a-front, and mainly thrust at me. I made me no more ado but took all their seven points in my target, thus.

Henry IV: Seven? Why, there were but four even now.

Falstaff: In buckram?

Edward Poins: Ay, four, in buckram suits.

Falstaff: Seven, by these hilts, or I am a villain else.

Prince Henry: I pray to thee, let him alone, we shall have more ah no.

Falstaff: Dost thou hear me, Hal?

Prince Henry: Ay, and mark thee too, Jack.

Falstaff: Do so, for it is worth the listening to. These nine in buckram that I told thee of…

Prince Henry: So, two more already.

Falstaff: Their points being broken.

Edward Poins: Down fell their hose.

Falstaff: Began to give me ground: but I followed me close, came in foot and hand, and with a thought seven of the eleven I paid.

Prince Henry: Oh monstrous! Eleven buckram men grown out of two!

Falstaff: But, as the devil would have it, three misbegotten knaves in Kendal green came at my back and let drive at me, for it was so dark, Hal, that thou couldst not see thy hand.

Prince Henry: These lies are like their father that begets them; gross as a mountain, open, palpable.

Why, thou clay-brained guts, thou knotty-pated fool, thou whoreson, obscene, grease tallow-catch…

Falstaff: What, art thou mad? art thou mad? Is not the truth the truth?

Prince Henry: Why, how couldst thou know these men in Kendal green, when it was so dark thou couldst not see thy hand?

Come, tell us your reason: what sayest thou to this?

Edward Poins: Come, your reason, Jack, your reason.

Falstaff: What, upon compulsion? And I were at the strappado, or all the racks in the world, I would not tell you on compulsion.

Give you a reason on compulsion! If reasons were as plentiful as blackberries, I would give no man a reason upon compulsion, I.

Prince Henry: I'll be no longer guilty of this sin, this sanguine coward, this bed-presser, this horseback-breaker, this huge hill of flesh…

Falstaff: It is blood, you starveling, you elf-skin, you dried neat's tongue, you bull's pizzle, you stock-fish!

Oh for breath to utter what is like thee! You tailor's-yard, you sheath, you bow case; you vile standing-tuck…

Prince Henry: Well, breathe awhile, and then to it again, and when thou hast tired thyself in base comparisons hear me speak but this.

Edward Poins: Mark, Jack.

Prince Henry: We two saw you four set on four and bound them, and were masters of their wealth.

Mark now how a plain tale shall put you down.

Then did we two set on you four, and with a word, out-faced you from your prize, and have it; yea and can show it you here in the house.

Falstaff, you carried your guts away as nimbly, with as quick dexterity, and roared for mercy and still run and roared, as ever I heard bull-calf.

What a slave art thou, to hack thy sword as thou hast done, and then say it was in fight!

What trick, what device, what starting-hole, canst thou now find out to hide thee from this open and apparent shame?

Edward Poins: Come, let's hear, Jack; what trick hast thou now?

Falstaff: By the Lord, I knew ye as well as he that made ye.

Why, hear you, my masters, was it for me to kill the heir-apparent? Should I turn upon the true prince?

Why, thou knowest I am as valiant as Hercules, but beware instinct, the lion will not touch the true prince.

Instinct is a great matter, I was now a coward on instinct.

I shall think the better of myself and thee during my life; I for a valiant lion, and thou for a true prince.

By the Lord lads, I am glad you have the money.

Hostess, clap to the doors, watch to-night, pray to-morrow.

Gallants lads, boys, hearts of gold, all the titles of good fellowship come to you!

What, shall we be merry? Shall we have a play extempore?

Prince Henry: Content; and the argument shall be thy running away.

Falstaff: Ah, no more of that, Hal, an thou lovest me!

(Hostess enters)

Hostess Quickly: Oh Jesus, my lord the prince!

Prince Henry: How now, my lady the hostess! What sayest thou to me?

Hostess Quickly: Marry, my lord, there is a nobleman of the court at door would speak with you.

He says he comes from your father.

Henry IV: Give him as much as will make him a royal man, and send him back again to my mother.

Falstaff: What manner of man is he?

Hostess Quickly: An old man.

Falstaff: What doth gravity out of his bed at midnight? Shall I give him his answer?

Prince Henry: I pray to the, do, Jack.

Falstaff: With faith, and I'll send him packing.

(Falstaff exits)

Prince Henry: Now, sirs: by'r lady, you fought fair; so did you Peto; so did you Bardolph.

You are lions too, you ran away upon instinct, you will not touch the true prince; no, fie!

Lord Bardolph: With faith, I ran when I saw others run.

Henry IV: With faith, tell me now in earnest, how came Falstaff's sword so hacked?

Peto: Why, he hacked it with his dagger, and said he would swear truth out of England but he would make you believe it was done in fight, and persuaded us to do the like.

Lord Bardolph: Yea, and to tickle our noses with spear-grass to make them bleed, and then to beslubber our garments with it and swear it was the blood of true men.

I did that I did not this seven year before, I blushed to hear his monstrous devices.

Prince Henry: Oh villain, thou stolest a cup of sack eighteen years ago, and wert taken with the manner, and ever since thou hast blushed extempore.

Thou hadst fire and sword on thy side, and yet thou rannest away.

What instinct hadst thou for it?

Lord Bardolph: My lord, do you see these meteors? Do you behold these exhalations?

Prince Henry: I do.

Lord Bardolph: What think you they portend?

Prince Henry: Hot livers and cold purses.

Lord Bardolph: Choler, my lord, if rightly taken.

Prince Henry: No, if rightly taken, halter. 1310

(Falstaff re-enters)

Here comes lean Jack, here comes bare-bone.

How now, my sweet creature of bombast!

How long is it ago Jack, since thou sawest thine own knee?

Falstaff: My own knee! When I was about thy years, Hal, I was not an eagle's talon in the waist; I could have crept into any alderman's thumb-ring.

A plague of sighing and grief! It blows a man up like a bladder.

There's villanous news abroad, here was Sir John Bracy from your father, you must to the court in the morning.

That same mad fellow of the north, Percy, and he of Wales, that gave Amamon the bastinado and made Lucifer cuckold and swore the devil his true liegeman upon the cross of a Welsh hook; what a plague call you him?

Edward Poins: Oh, Glendower.

Falstaff: Owen, Owen, the same, and his son-in-law Mortimer, and old Northumberland, and that sprightly Scot of Scots, Douglas, that runs on horseback up a hill perpendicular.

Prince Henry: He that rides at high speed and with his pistol kills a sparrow flying.

Falstaff: You have hit it.

Prince Henry: So did he never the sparrow.

Falstaff: Well, that rascal hath good mettle in him; he will not run.

Prince Henry: Why, what a rascal art thou then, to praise him so for running!

Falstaff: On horseback, ye cuckoo; but afoot he will not budge a foot.

Prince Henry: Yes, Jack, upon instinct.

Falstaff: I grant ye, upon instinct.

Well, he is there too, and one Mordake, and a thousand blue-caps more.

Worcester is stolen away to-night, thy father's beard is turned white with the news.

You may buy land now as cheap as stinking mackerel.

Prince Henry: Why, then, it is like, if there come a hot June and this civil buffeting hold, we shall buy maidenheads as they buy hobnails, by the hundreds.

Falstaff: By the mass, lad, thou sayest true; it is like we shall have good trading that way.

Tell me, Hal, art not thou horrible afeard? Thou being heir-apparent, could the world pick thee out three such enemies again as that fiend Douglas, that spirit Percy, and that devil Glendower?

Art thou not horribly afraid? Doth not thy blood thrill at it?

Prince Henry: Not a whit, in faith, I lack some of thy instinct.

Falstaff: Well, thou wert be horribly chid tomorrow when thou comest to thy father.

If thou love me, practise an answer.

Prince Henry: Do thou stand for my father, and examine me upon the particulars of my life.

Falstaff: Shall I? Content, this chair shall be my state, this dagger my sceptre, and this cushion my crown.

Prince Henry: Thy state is taken for a joined-stool, thy golden sceptre for a leaden dagger, and thy precious rich crown for a pitiful bald crown!

Falstaff: Well, and the fire of grace be not quite out of thee, now shalt thou be moved.

Give me a cup of sack to make my eyes look red, that it may be thought I have wept; for I must speak in passion, and I will do it in King Cambyses' vein.

Prince Henry: Well, here is my leg.

Falstaff: And here is my speech. Stand aside, nobility.

Hostess Quickly: Oh Jesus, this is excellent sport, in faith!

Falstaff: Weep not sweet queen, for trickling tears are vain.

Hostess Quickly: Oh the father, how he holds his countenance!

Falstaff: For God's sake, lords, convey my tristful queen; for tears do stop the flood-gates of her eyes.

Hostess Quickly: Oh Jesus, he doth it as like one of these harlotry players as ever I see!

Falstaff: Peace, good pint-pot; peace, good tickle-brain. 1380

Harry, I do not only marvel where thou spendest thy time, but also how thou art accompanied.

For though the camomile, the more it is trodden on the faster it grows, yet youth, the more it is wasted the sooner it wears.

That thou art my son, I have partly thy mother's word, partly my own opinion, but chiefly a villainous trick of thine eye and a foolish-hanging of thy nether lip, that doth warrant me.

If then thou be son to me, here lies the point; why, being son to me, art thou so pointed at?

Shall the blessed sun of heaven prove a micher and eat blackberries? A question not to be asked.

Shall the sun of England prove a thief and take purses? A question to be asked.

There is a thing, Harry, which thou hast often heard of and it is known to many in our land by the name of pitch.

This pitch, as ancient writers do report, doth defile, so doth the company thou keepest.

For, Harry, now I do not speak to thee in drink but in tears, not in pleasure but in passion, not in words only, but in woes also.

Yet there is a virtuous man whom I have often noted in thy company, but I know not his name.

Prince Henry: What manner of man, and it like your majesty?

Falstaff: A goodly portly man, in faith, and a corpulent, of a cheerful look, a pleasing eye and a most noble carriage; and as I think, his age some fifty, or by'r lady, inclining to three score; and now I remember me his name is Falstaff.

If that man should be lewdly given, he deceiveth me.

For Harry, I see virtue in his looks.

If then the tree may be known by the fruit, as the fruit by the tree, then, peremptorily I speak it, there is virtue in that Falstaff him keep with, the rest banish.

Tell me now, thou naughty varlet, tell me, where hast thou been this month?

Prince Henry: Dost thou speak like a king? Do thou stand for me, and I'll play my father.

Falstaff: Depose me? If thou dost it half so gravely, so majestically, both in word and matter, hang me up by the heels for a rabbit-sucker or a poulter's hare.

Prince Henry: Well, here I am set.

Falstaff: And here I stand: judge, my masters.

Prince Henry: Now, Harry, whence come you?

Falstaff: My noble lord, from Eastcheap.

Prince Henry: The complaints I hear of thee are grievous.

Falstaff: It is blood, my lord, they are false; nay I'll tickle ye for a young prince, in faith.

Prince Henry: Swearest thou, ungracious boy? Henceforth never look on me.

Thou art violently carried away from grace, there is a devil haunts thee in the likeness of an old fat man, a tun of man is thy companion.

Why dost thou converse with that trunk of humours, that bolting-hutch of beastliness, that swollen parcel of dropsies, that huge bombard of sack, that stuffed cloak-bag of guts, that roasted Manning tree ox with the pudding in his belly, that reverend vice, that grey iniquity, that father ruffian, that vanity in years?

Wherein is he good, but to taste sack and drink it? Wherein neat and cleanly, but to carve a capon and eat it?

Wherein cunning, but in craft? Wherein crafty, but in villainy?

Wherein villainous but in all things? Wherein worthy, but in nothing?

Falstaff: I would your grace would take me with you, whom means your grace?

Prince Henry: That villainous abominable misleader of youth, Falstaff, that old white-bearded Satan.

Falstaff: My lord, the man I know.

Prince Henry: I know thou dost.

Falstaff: But to say I know more harm in him than in myself, were to say more than I know.

That he is old, the more the pity, his white hairs do witness it; but that he is, saving your reverence, a whoremaster, that I utterly deny.

If sack and sugar be a fault, God help the wicked! If to be old and merry be a sin, then many an old host that I know is damned.

If to be fat be to be hated, then Pharaoh's lean kin are to be loved.

No, my good lord; banish Peto, banish Bardolph, banish Poins; but for sweet Jack

Falstaff, kind Jack Falstaff, true Jack Falstaff, valiant Jack Falstaff, and therefore more valiant, being, as he is old Jack Falstaff, banish not him thy Harry's company, banish not him thy Harry's company.

Banish plump Jack, and banish all the world.

Prince Henry: I do, I will.

(A knocking heard)

(Exeunt Hostess, Francis and Bardolph)

(Bardolph re-enters running)

Lord Bardolph: Oh my lord, my lord! The sheriff with a most monstrous watch is at the door.

Falstaff: Out, ye rogue! Play out the play, I have much to say in the behalf of that Falstaff.

(The Hostess re-enters)

Hostess Quickly: Oh Jesus, my lord, my lord!

Henry IV: Heigh, heigh! The devil rides upon a fiddlestick; what's the matter?

Hostess Quickly: The sheriff and all the watch are at the door, they are come to search the house.

Shall I let them in?

Falstaff: Dost thou hear, Hal? Never call a true piece of gold a counterfeit.

Thou art essentially mad, without seeming so.

Prince Henry: And thou a natural coward, without instinct.

Falstaff: I deny your major: if you will deny the sheriff, so, if not, let him enter.

If I become not a cart as well as another man, a plague on my bringing up!

I hope I shall as soon be strangled with a halter as another.

Prince Henry: Go, hide thee behind the arras, the rest walk up above.

Now, my masters, for a true face and good conscience.

Falstaff: Both which I have had: but their date is out, and therefore I'll hide me.

Prince Henry: Call in the Sheriff.

(Exeunt all except Prince Henry and Peto)

(Sheriff and the Carrier enter)

Now, master sheriff, what is your will with me?

Sheriff: First, pardon me, my lord. A hue and cry hath followed certain men unto this house.

Prince Henry: What men?

Sheriff: One of them is well known, my gracious lord, a gross fat man.

Carrier: As fat as butter.

Prince Henry: The man, I do assure you, is not here, for I myself at this time have employed him; and sheriff I will engage my word to thee that I will, by to-morrow dinner-time, send him to answer thee, or any man; for anything he shall be charged withal.

And so let me entreat you leave the house.

Sheriff: I will, my lord. There are two gentlemen

Have in this robbery lost three hundred marks.

Prince Henry: It may be so: if he have robb'd these men,

He shall be answerable; and so farewell.

Sheriff: Good night, my noble lord.

Prince Henry: I think it is good morrow, is it not?

Sheriff: Indeed, my lord, I think it be two o'clock.

(Exeunt Sheriff and Carrier)

Henry IV: This oily rascal is known as well as Paul's.

Go, call him forth.

Peto: Falstaff!

Fast asleep behind the arras, and snorting like a horse.

Prince Henry: Hark, how hard he fetches breath.

Search his pockets.

(He searcheth his pockets, and findeth certain papers)

What hast thou found?

Peto: Nothing but papers, my lord.

Prince Henry: Let's see what they be, read them.

Peto: (Reads)

Items: A sack of capon, two gallons of sauce, sack of anchovies, bread.

Prince Henry: Oh monstrous! But one half-penny-worth of bread to this intolerable deal of sack!

What there is else, keep close; we'll read it at more advantage.

There, let him sleep till day, I'll to the court in the morning.

We must all to the wars, and thy place shall be honourable, I'll procure this fat rogue a charge of foot; and I know his death will be a march of twelve-score.

The money shall be paid back again with advantage.

Be with me betimes in the morning, and so, good morrow Peto.

(Exeunt)

Peto: Good morrow, good my lord.

Act III, Scene 1

The Archdeacon's house. (Bangor)

(Hotspur, Worcester, Mortimer, and Glendower enter)

Mortimer: These promises are fair, the parties sure, and our induction full of prosperous hope.

Hotspur (Henry Percy): Lord Mortimer, and cousin Glendower, will you sit down?

Uncle Worcester: A plague upon it! I have forgot the map.

Glendower: No, here it is.

Sit, cousin Percy, sit; good cousin Hotspur for by that name as often as Lancaster doth speak of you, his cheek looks pale and with a rising sigh he wisheth you in heaven.

Hotspur (Henry Percy): And you in hell, as oft as he hears Owen Glendower spoke of.

Glendower: I cannot blame him, at my nativity the front of heaven was full of fiery shapes, of burning cressets; and at my birth the frame and huge foundation of the earth shaked like a coward.

Hotspur (Henry Percy): Why, so it would have done at the same season, if your mother's cat had but kittened, though yourself had never been born.

Glendower: I say the earth did shake when I was born.

Hotspur (Henry Percy): And I say the earth was not of my mind, if you suppose as fearing you it shook.

Glendower: The heavens were all on fire, the earth did tremble.

Hotspur (Henry Percy): Oh, then the earth shook to see the heavens on fire, and not in fear of your nativity.

Diseased nature oftentimes breaks forth in strange eruptions, often the teeming earth is with a kind of colic pinched and vexed by the imprisoning of unruly wind within her womb; which for enlargement striving shakes the old beldam earth and topples down steeples and moss-grown towers.

At your birth our grandam earth, having this distemperature, in passion shook.

Glendower: Cousin, of many men I do not bear these crossings.

Give me leave to tell you once again that at my birth the front of heaven was full of fiery shapes, the goats ran from the mountains, and the herds were strangely clamorous to the frighted fields.

These signs have marked me extraordinary, and all the courses of my life do show I am not in the roll of common men.

Where is he living, clipped in with the sea that chides the banks of England, Scotland, Wales, which calls me pupil, or hath read to me?

Bring him out that is but woman's son can trace me in the tedious ways of art and hold me pace in deep experiments.

Hotspur (Henry Percy): I think there's no man speaks better Welsh.

I'll to dinner.

Mortimer: Peace, cousin Percy, you will make him mad.

Glendower: I can call spirits from the vasty deep.

Hotspur (Henry Percy): Why, so can I, or so can any man, but will they come when you do call for them?

Glendower: Why, I can teach you, cousin, to command the devil.

Hotspur (Henry Percy): I can teach thee, coz, to shame the devil by telling truth.

Tell truth and shame the devil.

If thou have power to raise him, bring him hither and I'll be sworn I have power to shame him hence.

Oh, while you live, tell truth and shame the devil!

Mortimer: Come, come, no more of this unprofitable chat.

Glendower: Three times hath Henry Bolingbroke made head against my power; thrice from the banks of Wye and sandy-bottomed Severn have I sent him bootless home and weather-beaten back.

Hotspur (Henry Percy): Home without boots, and in foul weather too!

How escapes he agues, in the devil's name?

Glendower: Come, here's the map, shall we divide our right according to our threefold order taken?

Mortimer: The archdeacon hath divided it into three limits very equally.

England from Trent and Severn hitherto by south and east is to my part assigned, all westward and Wales beyond the Severn shore, all the fertile land within that bound to Owen Glendower; and dear coz, to you the remnant northward, lying off from Trent.

Our indentures tripartite are drawn, which being sealed interchangeably, a business that this night may execute, to-morrow, cousin Percy, you and I and my good Lord of Worcester will set forth to meet your father and the Scottish power as is appointed us, at Shrewsbury.

My father Glendower is not ready yet, nor shall we need his help these fourteen days.

Within that space you may have drawn together your tenants, friends and neighbouring gentlemen.

Glendower: A shorter time shall send me to you lords, and in my conduct shall your ladies come; from whom you now must steal and take no leave, for there will be a world of water shed upon the parting of your wives and you.

Hotspur (Henry Percy): Methinks my moiety, north from Burton here in quantity equals not one of yours.

See how this river comes me cranking in, and cuts me from the best of all my land a huge half-moon, a monstrous cantle out.

I'll have the current in this place dammed up, and here the smug and silver Trent shall run in a new channel, fair and evenly; it shall not wind with such a deep indent to rob me of so rich a bottom here.

Glendower: Not wind? It shall, it must, you see it doth.

Mortimer: Yea, but Mark how he bears his course and runs me up with like advantage on the other side; Gelding the opposed continent as much as on the other side it takes from you.

Earl of Worcester: Yea, but a little charge will trench him here and on this north side win this cape of land, and then he runs straight and even.

Hotspur (Henry Percy): I'll have it so: a little charge will do it.

Glendower: I'll not have it altered.

Hotspur (Henry Percy): Will not you?

Glendower: No, nor you shall not.

Hotspur (Henry Percy): Who shall say me nay?

Glendower: Why, that will I.

Hotspur (Henry Percy): Let me not understand you, then; speak it in Welsh.

Glendower: I can speak English, lord, as well as you for I was trained up in the English court; where being but young, I framed to the harp many an English ditty lovely well and gave the tongue a helpful ornament, a virtue that was never seen in you.

Hotspur (Henry Percy): Merrily, and I am glad of it with all my heart, I had rather be a kitten and cry mew than one of these same metre ballad-mongers; I had rather hear a brazen canstick turned, or a dry wheel grate on the axle-tree, and that would set my teeth nothing on edge, nothing so much as mincing poetry.

It is like the forced gait of a shuffling nag.

Glendower: Come, you shall have Trent turned.

Hotspur (Henry Percy): I do not care, I'll give thrice so much land To any well-deserving friend, but in the way of bargain, mark ye me, I'll cavil on the ninth part of a hair.

Are the indentures drawn? Shall we be gone?

Glendower: The moon shines fair; you may away by night, I'll haste the writer and withal break with your wives of your departure hence.

I am afraid my daughter will run mad, so much she doteth on her Mortimer.

(Glendower exits)

Mortimer: Fie, cousin Percy! How you cross my father!

Hotspur (Henry Percy): I cannot choose: sometime he angers me with telling me of the mouldwarp and the ant, of the dreamer Merlin and his prophecies, and of a dragon and a finless fish.

A clip-wing'd griffin and a moulten raven, a couching lion and a ramping cat, and such a deal of skimble-skamble stuff as puts me from my faith.

I tell you what, he held me last night at least nine hours in reckoning up the several devils' names that were his lackeys.

I cried: hum, and well go to, but marked him not a word.

Oh, he is as tedious as a tired horse, a railing wife, worse than a smoky house, I had rather live with cheese and garlic in a windmill, far, than feed on cates and have him talk to me in any summer-house in Christendom.

Mortimer: In faith he is a worthy gentleman, exceedingly well read and profited in strange concealments, valiant as a lion and as wondrous affable and as bountiful as mines of India.

Shall I tell you, cousin? He holds your temper in a high respect and curbs himself even of his natural scope when you come across his humour; faith he does.

I warrant you, that man is not alive might so have tempted him as you have done, without the taste of danger and reproof, but do not use it often, let me entreat you.

Earl of Worcester: In faith my lord, you are too wilful-blame, and since your coming hither have done enough to put him quite beside his patience.

You must needs learn, lord, to amend this fault, though sometimes it show greatness, courage, blood, and that's the dearest grace it renders you; yet oftentimes it doth present harsh rage, defect of manners, want of government, pride, haughtiness, opinion and disdain.

The least of which haunting a nobleman loseth men's hearts and leaves behind a stain upon the beauty of all parts besides, beguiling them of commendation.

Hotspur (Henry Percy): Well, I am schooled, good manners be your speed!

Here come our wives, and let us take our leave.

(Glendower re-enters with the ladies)

Mortimer: This is the deadly spite that angers me, y wife can speak no English, I know Welsh.

Glendower: My daughter weeps: she will not part with you, she'll be a soldier too, she'll to the wars.

Mortimer: Good father, tell her that she and my aunt Percy shall follow in your conduct speedily.

(Glendower speaks to her in Welsh, and she answers him in the same)

Glendower: She is desperate here; a peevish self-wind harlotry, one that no persuasion can do good upon.

(The lady speaks in Welsh)

Mortimer: I understand thy looks, that pretty Welsh which thou pour'st down from these swelling heavens, I am too perfect in and but for shame in such a parley should I answer thee.

(The lady speaks again in Welsh)

I understand thy kisses and thou mine, and that's a feeling disputation, but I will never be a truant love, till I have learned thy language; for thy tongue makes Welsh as sweet as ditties highly penned, sung by a fair queen in a summer's bower with ravishing division to her lute.

Glendower: Nay, if you melt, then will she run mad.

(The lady speaks again in Welsh)

Mortimer: Oh, I am ignorance itself in this!

Glendower: She bids you on the wanton rushes lay you down and rest your gentle head upon her lap, and she will sing the song that pleaseth you, and on your eyelids crown the god of sleep.

Charming your blood with pleasing heaviness, making such difference it twist wake and sleep, as is the difference betwixt day and night the hour before the heavenly-harnessed team begins his golden progress in the east.

Mortimer: With all my heart I'll sit and hear her sing by that time will our book, I think, be drawn

Glendower: Do so, and those musicians that shall play to you hang in the air a thousand leagues from hence, and straight they shall be here: sit, and attend.

Hotspur (Henry Percy): Come Kate, thou art perfect in lying down, come quick; quick, that I may lay my head in thy lap.

Lady Percy: Go, ye giddy goose.

(The music plays)

Hotspur (Henry Percy): Now I perceive the devil understands Welsh, and it is no marvel he is so humorous.

By'r lady, he is a good musician.

Lady Percy: Then should you be nothing but musical for you are altogether governed by humours.

Lie still, ye thief, and hear the lady sing in Welsh.

Hotspur (Henry Percy): I had rather hear Lady, my brach, howl in Irish.

Lady Percy: Wouldst thou have thy head broken?

Hotspur (Henry Percy): No.

Lady Percy: Then be still.

Hotspur (Henry Percy): Neither; it is a woman's fault.

Lady Percy: Now God help thee!

Hotspur (Henry Percy): To the Welsh lady's bed.

Lady Percy: What's that?

Hotspur (Henry Percy): Peace! She sings.

(Here the lady sings a Welsh song)

Hotspur (Henry Percy): Come Kate, I'll have your song too.

Lady Percy: Not mine, in good sooth.

Hotspur (Henry Percy): Not yours, in good sooth! Heart! you swear like a comfit-maker's wife.

Not you, in good sooth, and as true as I live, and as God shall mend me, and as sure as day, and givest such sarcenet surety for thy oaths; as if thou never walk'st further than Finsbury.

Swear me Kate, like a lady as thou art, a good mouth-filling oath, and leave in sooth, and such protest of pepper-gingerbread, to velvet-guards and Sunday-citizens.

Come, sing.

Lady Percy: I will not sing.

Hotspur (Henry Percy): It is the next way to turn tailor, or be red-breast teacher.

An the indentures be drawn, I'll away within these two hours; and so come in when ye will.

(Exit)

Glendower: Come, come, Lord Mortimer; you are as slow as hot Lord Percy is on fire to go.

By this our book is drawn, we'll but seal, and then to horse immediately.

Mortimer: With all my heart.

(Exeunt)

Act III, Scene 2

The palace. (London)

(King Henry IV, Prince Henry, and others enter)

Prince Henry: Lords, give us leave; the Prince of Wales and I must have some private conference; but be near at hand, for we shall presently have need of you.

(Exeunt Lords)

I know not whether God will have it so, for some displeasing service I have done that in his secret doom, out of my blood, he will breed revengement and a scourge for me; but thou dost in thy passages of life make me believe that thou art only mark'd for the hot vengeance and the rod of heaven to punish my mistreadings.

Tell me else, could such inordinate and low desires, such poor, such bare, such lewd, such mean attempts; such barren pleasures, rude society as thou art matched withal and grafted to, accompany the greatness of thy blood and hold their level with thy princely heart?

Henry IV: So please your majesty, I would I could quit all offences with as clear excuse as well as I am doubtless I can purge myself of many I am charged withal: yet such extenuation let me beg, as in reproof of many tales devised; which often the ear of greatness needs must hear by smiling pick-thanks and base news-mongers.

I may, for some things true, wherein my youth hath faulty wandered and irregular, find pardon on my true submission.

Prince Henry: God pardon thee! yet let me wonder, Harry, at thy affections which do hold a wing quite from the flight of all thy ancestors.

Thy place in council thou hast rudely lost, which by thy younger brother is supplied, and art almost an alien to the hearts of all the court and princes of my blood.

The hope and expectation of thy time is ruined, and the soul of every man prophetically doth forethink thy fall.

Had I so lavish of my presence been, so common-hackneyed in the eyes of men, so stale and cheap to vulgar company opinion, that did help me to the crown had still kept loyal to possession and left me in reputeless banishment a fellow of no mark, nor likelihood.

By being seldom seen, I could not stir but like a comet I was wondered at, that men would tell their children: This is he.

Others would say Where, which is Bolingbroke? And then I stole all courtesy from heaven and dressed myself in such humility that I did pluck allegiance from men's hearts; loud shouts and salutations from their mouths, even in the presence of the crowned king.

Thus did I keep my person fresh and new, my presence like a robe pontifical, never seen but wondered at; and so my state seldom but sumptuous, showed like a feast and won by rareness such solemnity.

The skipping king, he ambled up and down with shallow jesters and rash bavin wits, soon kindled and soon burnt; carded his state, mingled his royalty with capering fools had his great name profaned with their scorns, and gave his countenance against his name; to laugh at gibing boys and stand the push of every beardless vain comparative, grew a companion to the common streets, enfeoffed himself to popularity,

That, being daily swallowed by men's eyes, they surfeited with honey and began to loathe the taste of sweetness, whereof a little more than a little is by much too much.

So when he had occasion to be seen, he was but as the cuckoo is in June heard not, regarded seen, but with such eyes as sick and blunted with community; afford no extraordinary gaze such as is bent on sun-like majesty when it shines seldom in admiring eyes.

But rather drowzed and hung their eyelids down, slept in his face and rendered such aspect as cloudy men use to their adversaries, being with his presence glutted, gorged and full, and in that very line

Harry, standest thou; for thou has lost thy princely privilege with vile participation.

Not an eye, but is a-weary of thy common sight, save mine; which hath desired to see thee more, which now doth that I would not have it do, make blind itself with foolish tenderness.

Henry IV: I shall hereafter, my thrice gracious lord, be more myself.

Prince Henry: For all the world ,as thou art to this hour was Richard then when I from France set foot at Ravenspurgh, and even as I was then is Percy now.

Now, by my sceptre and my soul to boot, he hath more worthy interest to the state than thou the shadow of succession; for of no right, nor colour like to right, he doth fill fields with harness in the realm turns head against the lion's armed jaws, and being no more in debt to years than thou leads ancient lords and reverend bishops on to bloody battles and to bruising arms.

What never-dying honour hath he got against renowned Douglas!

Whose high deeds, whose hot incursions and great name in arms holds from all soldiers chief majority, and military title capital through all the kingdoms that acknowledge Christ.

Thrice hath this Hotspur, Mars in swathling clothes, this infant warrior in his enterprises discomfited great Douglas, taken him once, enlarged him and made a friend of him to fill the mouth of deep defiance up and shake the peace and safety of our throne.

And what say you to this? Percy, Northumberland, the Archbishop's grace of York, Douglas, Mortimer, Capitulate against us and are up; but wherefore do I tell these news to thee?

Why, Harry, do I tell thee of my foes, which art my near'st and dearest enemy?

Thou that art like enough, through vassal fear, base inclination and the start of spleen to fight against me under Percy's pay to dog his heels and curtsy at his frowns, to show how much thou art degenerate.

Henry IV: Do not think so; you shall not find it so, and God forgive them that so much have swayed your majesty's good thoughts away from me!

I will redeem all this on Percy's head and in the closing of some glorious day be bold to tell you that I am your son; when I will wear a garment all of blood and stain my favours in a bloody mask, which washed away shall scour my shame with it.

That shall be the day, whene'er it lights, that this same child of honour and renown, this gallant Hotspur, this all-praised knight, and your unthought-of Harry chance to meet.

For every honour sitting on his helm, would they were multitudes, and on my head my shames redoubled! For the time will come, that I shall make this northern youth exchange his glorious deeds for my indignities.

Percy is but my factor, good my lord, to engross up glorious deeds on my behalf, and I will call him to so strict account, that he shall render every glory up; yea, even the slightest worship of his time, or I will tear the reckoning from his heart.

This, in the name of God, I promise here, the which if He be pleased I shall perform, I do beseech your majesty may salve the long-grown wounds of my intemperance.

If not, the end of life cancels all bands, and I will die a hundred thousand deaths here break the smallest parcel of this vow.

Prince Henry: A hundred thousand rebels die in this, thou shalt have charge and sovereign trust herein.

(Blunt enters)

How now, good Blunt? Thy looks are full of speed.

Blunt: So hath the business that I come to speak of.

Lord Mortimer of Scotland hath sent word that Douglas and the English rebels met the eleventh of this month at Shrewsbury, a mighty and a fearful head they are, if promises be kept on every hand as ever offered foul play in the state.

Henry IV: The Earl of Westmoreland set forth to-day, with him my son, Lord John of Lancaster, for this advertisement is five days old.

On Wednesday next, Harry, you shall set forward, on Thursday we ourselves will march.

Our meeting is Bridgenorth, and Harry you shall march through Gloucestershire, by which account our business valued, some twelve days hence our general forces at Bridgenorth shall meet.

Our hands are full of business, let's away, advantage feeds him fat while men delay. **(Exeunt)**

Act III, Scene 3

The Boar's-Head Tavern. (Eastcheap)

(Falstaff and Bardolph enter)

Falstaff: Bardolph, am I not fallen away vilely since this last action? Do I not bate?

Do I not dwindle? Why my skin hangs about me like an like an old lady's loose gown; I am withered like an old apple-john.

Well, I'll repent, and that suddenly, while I am in some liking; I shall be out of heart shortly, and then I shall have no strength to repent.

Ad I have not forgotten what the inside of a church is made of, I am a peppercorn, a brewer's horse.

The inside of a church! Company, villanous company, hath been the spoil of me.

Lord Bardolph: Sir John, you are so fretful, you cannot live long.

Falstaff: Why, there is it: come sing me a bawdy song, make me merry. I was as virtuously given as a gentleman need to be; virtuous enough, swore little, diced not above seven times a week, went to a bawdy-house once in a quarter; of an hour paid money that I borrowed, three of four times, lived well and in good compass.

And now I live out of all order, out of all compass.

Lord Bardolph: Why, you are so fat, Sir John, that you must needs be out of all compass, out of all reasonable compass, Sir John.

Falstaff: Do thou amend thy face, and I'll amend my life.

Thou art our admiral, thou bearest the lantern in the poop, but it is in the nose of thee. thou art the Knight of the Burning Lamp.

Lord Bardolph: Why, Sir John, my face does you no harm.

Falstaff: No, I'll be sworn, I make as good use of it as many a man doth of a Death's-head or a memento mori.

I never see thy face but I think upon hell-fire and Dives that lived in purple; for there he is in his robes, burning, burning.

If thou wert any way given to virtue, I would swear by thy face; my oath should be: By this fire, that's God's angel, but thou art altogether given over, and wert indeed, but for the light in thy face, the son of utter darkness.

When thou rannest up Gadshill in the night to catch my horse, if I did not think thou hadst been an ignis fatuus or a ball of wildfire, there's no purchase in money.

Oh thou art a perpetual triumph, an everlasting bonfire-light!

Thou hast saved me a thousand marks in links and torches, walking with thee in the night between tavern and tavern, but the sack that thou hast drunk me would have bought me lights as good cheap at the dearest chandler's in Europe.

I have maintained that salamander of yours with fire any time this two and thirty years; God reward me for it!

Lord Bardolph: It is blood, I would my face were in your belly!

Falstaff: God-a-mercy! So should I be sure to be heart-burned.

(Enter Hostess)

How now, Dame Partlet the hen! Have you inquired yet who picked my pocket?

Hostess Quickly: Why, Sir John, what do you think, Sir John?

Do you think I keep thieves in my house? I have searched, I have inquired, so has my husband, man by man, boy by boy, servant by servant: the tithe of a hair was never lost in my house before.

Falstaff: Ye lie, hostess: Bardolph was shaved and lost many a hair, and I'll be sworn my pocket was picked.

Go to, you are a woman, go.

Hostess Quickly: Who I? No, I defy thee.

God's light, I was never called so in mine own house before.

Falstaff: Go to, I know you well enough.

Hostess Quickly: No, Sir John, you do not know me, Sir John.

I know you, Sir John, you owe me money, Sir John, and now you pick a quarrel to beguile me of it.

I bought you a dozen of shirts to your back.

Falstaff: Dowlas, filthy dowlas: I have given them away to bakers' wives, and they have made bolters of them.

Hostess Quickly: Now, as I am a true woman, holland of eight shillings an ell.

You owe money here besides, Sir John, for your diet and by-drinkings, and money lent you, four and twenty pound.

Falstaff: He had his part of it; let him pay.

Hostess Quickly: He? Alas, he is poor; he hath nothing.

Falstaff: How! poor? Look upon his face; what call you rich?

Let them coin his nose, let them coin his cheeks, Ill not pay a denier.

What, will you make a younker of me?

Shall I not take mine case in mine inn but I shall have my pocket picked?

I have lost a seal-ring of my grandfather's worth forty mark.

Hostess Quickly: Oh Jesus, I have heard the prince tell him, I know not how often, that ring was copper!

Falstaff: How! the prince is a Jack, a sneak-cup, it is blood, an he were here, I would cudgel him like a dog, if he would say so.

(Prince Henry and Peto enter marching, and Falstaff meets them playing on his truncheon like a life)

How now, lad! is the wind in that door, in faith? Must we all march?

Lord Bardolph: Yea, two and two, Newgate fashion.

Hostess Quickly: My lord, I pray you, hear me.

Prince Henry: What sayest thou, Mistress Quickly? How doth thy husband?

I love him well; he is an honest man.

Hostess Quickly: Good my lord, hear me.

Falstaff: I pray to thee, let her alone, and list to me.

Prince Henry: What sayest thou, Jack?

Falstaff: The other night I fell asleep here behind the arras and had my pocket picked: this house is turned bawdy-house; they pick pockets.

Prince Henry: What didst thou lose, Jack?

Falstaff: Wilt thou believe me, Hal? Three or four bonds of forty pound apiece, and a seal-ring of my grandfather's.

Prince Henry: A trifle, some eight-penny matter.

Hostess Quickly: So I told him, my lord, and I said I heard your grace say so; and my lord, he speaks most vilely of you, like a foul-mouthed man as he is, and said he would cudgel you.

Prince Henry: What! He did not?

Hostess Quickly: There's neither faith, truth, nor womanhood in me else.

Falstaff: There's no more faith in thee than in a stewed prune, nor no more truth in thee than in a drawn fox, and for womanhood, Maid Marian may be the deputy's wife of the ward to thee.

Go, you thing, go

Hostess Quickly: Say, what thing? What thing?

Falstaff: What thing! Why, a thing to thank God on.

Hostess Quickly: I am no thing to thank God on, I would thou shouldst know it; I am an honest man's wife, and setting thy knighthood aside, thou art a knave to call me so.

Falstaff: Setting thy womanhood aside, thou art a beast to say otherwise.

Hostess Quickly: Say, what beast, thou knave, thou?

Falstaff: What beast! Why an otter.

Prince Henry: An otter, Sir John! Why an otter?

Falstaff: Why, she's neither fish nor flesh; a man knows not where to have her.

Hostess Quickly: Thou art an unjust man in saying so, thou or any man knows where to have me, thou knave, thou!

Henry IV: Thou sayest true, hostess; and he slanders thee most grossly.

Hostess Quickly: So he doth you, my lord, and said this other day you ought him a thousand pound.

Prince Henry: Sirrah, do I owe you a thousand pound?

Falstaff: A thousand pound, Ha! a million: thy love is worth a million, thou owest me thy love.

Hostess Quickly: Nay, my lord, he called you Jack and said he would cudgel you.

Falstaff: Did I, Bardolph?

Lord Bardolph: Indeed, Sir John, you said so.

Falstaff: Yea, if he said my ring was copper.

Prince Henry: I say it is copper, darest thou be as good as thy word now?

Falstaff: Why Hal, thou knowest as thou art but man, I dare, but as thou art prince, I fear thee as I fear the roaring of a lion's whelp.

Prince Henry: And why not as the lion?

Falstaff: The king is to be feared as the lion: dost thou think I'll fear thee as I fear thy father? Nay, and I do, I pray God my girdle break.

Prince Henry: Oh if it should, how would thy guts fall about thy knees! But, sirrah there's no room for faith, truth, nor honesty in this bosom of thine; it is all filled up with guts and midriff.

Charge an honest woman with picking thy pocket! Why thou whoreson, impudent, embossed rascal, if there were anything in thy pocket but tavern-reckonings, memorandums of bawdy-houses, and one poor penny-worth of sugar-candy to make thee long-winded, if thy pocket were enriched with any other injuries but these am a villain.

Yet you will stand to if, you will not pocket up wrong: art thou not ashamed?

Falstaff: Dost thou hear, Hal? Thou knowest in the state of innocency Adam fell; and what should poor Jack Falstaff do in the days of villany?

Thou seest I have more flesh than another man, and therefore more frailty.

You confess then, you picked my pocket?

Prince Henry: It appears so by the story.

Falstaff: Hostess I forgive thee, go, make ready breakfast love thy husband; look to thy servants, cherish thy guests.

Thou shalt find me tractable to any honest reason, thou seest I am pacified still.

Nay, pray to thee, be gone.

(Hostess exits)

Now Hal, to the news at court: for the robbery, lad, how is that answered?

Prince Henry: Oh my sweet beef, I must still be good angel to thee, the money is paid back again.

Falstaff: Oh I do not like that paying back; it is a double labour.

Prince Henry: I am good friends with my father and may do anything.

Falstaff: Rob me the exchequer the first thing thou doest, and do it with unwashed hands too.

Lord Bardolph: Do, my lord.

Prince Henry: I have procured thee, Jack, a charge of foot.

Falstaff: I would it had been of horse.

Where shall I find one that can steal well? Oh for a fine thief, of the age of two and twenty or thereabouts!

I am heinously unprovided.

Well, God be thanked for these rebels, they offend none but the virtuous, I laud them, I praise them.

Henry IV: Bardolph!

Lord Bardolph: My lord?

Henry IV: Go bear this letter to Lord John of Lancaster, to my brother John, this to my Lord of Westmoreland.

(Bardolph exits)

Go, Peto, to horse, to horse, for thou and I have thirty miles to ride yet here dinner time.

(Exit Peto)

Jack, meet me to-morrow in the temple hall at two o'clock in the afternoon.

There shalt thou know thy charge, and there receive Money, and order for their furniture.

The land is burning, Percy stands on high, and either we or they must lower lie.

(Prince Henry exits)

Falstaff: Rare words! brave world! Hostess, my breakfast, come!

Oh I could wish this tavern were my drum!

(Exits)

Act IV, Scene 1

The rebel camp near Shrewsbury.

(Hotspur, Worcester, and Douglas enter)

Hotspur (Henry Percy): Well said, my noble Scot, if speaking truth in this fine age were not thought flattery, such attribution should the Douglas have.

As not a soldier of this season's stamp should go so general current through the world.

By God, I cannot flatter, I do defy the tongues of soothers, but a braver place in my heart's love hath no man than yourself.

Nay, task me to my word, approve me lord.

Earl of Douglas: Thou art the king of honour, no man so potent breathes upon the ground, but I will beard him.

Hotspur (Henry Percy): Do so, and it is well.

(A Messenger enters with letters)

What letters hast thou there? I can but thank you.

Messenger: These letters come from your father.

Hotspur (Henry Percy): Letters from him! Why comes he not himself?

Messenger: He cannot come, my lord; he is grievous sick.

Hotspur (Henry Percy): How has he the leisure to be sick in such a rustling time?

Who leads his power?

Under whose government come they along?

Messenger: His letters bear his mind, not I, my lord.

Earl of Worcester: I pray to thee, tell me, doth he keep his bed?

Messenger: He did, my lord, four days ere I set forth, and at the time of my departure thence; he was much feared by his physicians.

Earl of Worcester: I would the state of time had first been whole were he by sickness had been visited.

His health was never better worth than now.

Hotspur (Henry Percy): Sick now! Droop now! This sickness doth infect the very life-blood of our enterprise; it is catching hither, even to our camp.

He writes me here, that inward sickness, and that his friends by deputation could not so soon be drawn, nor did he think it meet to lay so dangerous and dear a trust on any soul removed but on his own.

Yet doth he give us bold advertisement, that with our small conjunction we should on, to see how fortune is disposed to us; for as he writes, there is no quailing now.

Because the king is certainly possessed, of all our purposes. What say you to it?

Earl of Worcester: Your father's sickness is a maim to us.

Hotspur (Henry Percy): A perilous gash, a very limb lopp'd off; and yet, in faith, it is not, his present want aeems more than we shall find it.

Were it good to set the exact wealth of all our states all at one cast?

To set so rich a main on the nice hazard of one doubtful hour?

It were not good; for therein should we read the very bottom and the soul of hope, the very list, the very utmost bound of all our fortunes.

Earl of Douglas: In Faith, and so we should, where now remains a sweet reversion.

We may boldly spend upon the hope of what is to come in.

A comfort of retirement lives in this.

Hotspur (Henry Percy): A rendezvous, a home to fly unto.

If that the devil and mischance look big upon the maidenhead of our affairs.

Earl of Worcester: But yet I would your father had been here.

The quality and hair of our attempt brooks no division.

It will be thought by some, that know not why he is away; that wisdom, loyalty and mere dislike of our proceedings kept the earl from hence.

Think how such an apprehension may turn the tide of fearful faction and breed a kind of question in our cause; for well you know we of the offering side must keep aloof from strict arbitrement, and stop all sight-holes, every loop from whence the eye of reason may pry in upon us.

This absence of your father's draws a curtain that shows the ignorant a kind of fear before not dreamt of.

Hotspur (Henry Percy): You strain too far.

I rather of his absence make this use, it lends a lustre and more great opinion, a larger dare to our great enterprise; than if the earl were here for men must think.

If we without his help can make a head to push against a kingdom with his help, we shall overturn it topsy-turvy down.

Yet all goes well, yet all our joints are whole.

Earl of Douglas: As heart can think: there is not such a word spoke of in Scotland as this term of fear.

(Sir Richard Vernon enters)

Hotspur (Henry Percy): My cousin Vernon, welcome, by my soul.

Vernon: Pray God my news be worth a welcome, lord.

The Earl of Westmoreland is marching hitherwards seven thousand strong with him Prince John.

Hotspur (Henry Percy): No harm, what more?

Vernon: And further, I have learned, the king himself in person is set forth, or hitherwards intended speedily with strong and mighty preparation.

Hotspur (Henry Percy): He shall be welcome too.

Where is his son, the nimble-footed madcap Prince of Wales and his comrades, that daffed the world aside, and bid it pass?

Vernon: All furnished, all in arms, all plumed like estridges that with the wind baited like eagles having lately bathed; glittering in golden coats, like image; as full of spirit as the month of May, and gorgeous as the sun at midsummer, Wanton as youthful goats, wild as young bulls.

I saw young Harry, with his beaver on, his cuisses on his thighs, gallantly armed, rise from the ground like feathered Mercury, and vaulted with such ease into his seat as if an angel dropped down from the clouds; to turn and wind a fiery Pegasus and witch the world with noble horsemanship.

Hotspur (Henry Percy): No more, no more: worse than the sun in March, this praise doth nourish agues.

Let them come, they come like sacrifices in their trim, and to the fire-eyed maid of smoky war all hot and bleeding will we offer them.

The mailed Mars shall on his altar sit up to the ears in blood.

I am on fire to hear this rich reprisal is so nigh, and yet not ours.

Come, let me taste my horse, who is to bear me like a thunderbolt against the bosom of the Prince of Wales.

Harry to Harry shall, hot horse to horse, meet and never part till one drop down a corpse.

Oh that Glendower were come!

Vernon: There is more news, I learned in Worcester, as I rode along, he cannot draw his power this fourteen days.

Earl of Douglas: That's the worst tidings that I hear of yet.

Earl of Worcester: Ay, by my faith, that bears a frosty sound.

Hotspur (Henry Percy): What may the king's whole battle reach unto?

Vernon: To thirty thousand.

Hotspur (Henry Percy): Forty let it be, my father and Glendower being both away, the powers of us may serve so great a day

Come, let us take a muster speedily, doomsday is near; die all, die merrily.

Earl of Douglas: Talk not of dying: I am out of fear of death or death's hand for this one-half year.   **(Exeunt)**

Act IV, Scene 2

A public road near Coventry.

(Falstaff and Bardolph enter)

Falstaff: Bardolph, get thee before to Coventry, fill me a bottle of sack.

Our soldiers shall march through, we'll to Sutton Co'fil tonight.

Lord Bardolph: Will you give me money, captain?

Falstaff: Lay out, lay out.

Lord Bardolph: This bottle makes an angel.

Falstaff: An if it do, take it for thy labour and if it make twenty, take them all; I'll answer the coinage.

Bid my lieutenant Peto meet me at town's end.

Lord Bardolph: I will, captain.

farewell.

(Exits)

Falstaff: If I be not ashamed of my soldiers, I am a soused gurnet.

I have misused the king's press damnably.

I have got, in exchange of a hundred and fifty soldiers, three hundred and odd pounds.

I press me none but good house-holders, yeoman's sons inquire me out contracted bachelors, such as had been asked twice on the banns; such a commodity of warm slaves, as had as pound hear the devil as a drum, such as fear the report of a caliver worse than a struck fowl or a hurt wild-duck.

I pressed me none but such toasts-and-butter, with hearts in their bellies no bigger than pins' heads, and they have bought out their services; and now my whole charge consists of ancients, corporals, lieutenants, gentlemen of companies, slaves as ragged as Lazarus in the painted cloth, where the glutton's dogs licked his sores; and such as indeed were never soldiers, but discarded unjust serving-men, younger sons to younger brothers, revolted tapsters and ostlers trade-fallen, the cankers of a calm world and a long peace ten times more dishonourable ragged than an old faced ancient.

And such have I, to fill up the rooms of them that have bought out their services, that you would think that I had a hundred and fifty tattered prodigals lately come from swine-keeping, from eating draff and husks.

A mad fellow met me on the way and told me I had unloaded all the gibbets and pressed the dead bodies.

No eye hath seen such scarecrows.

I'll not march through coventry with them, that's flat.

Nay, and the villains march wide betwixt the legs, as if they had gyves on; for indeed I had the most of them out of prison.

There's but a shirt and a half in all my company; and the half shirt is two napkins tacked together and thrown over the shoulders like an herald's coat without sleeves; and the shirt, to say the truth, stolen from my host at Saint Alban's, or the red-nose innkeeper of Daventry.

That's all one; they'll find linen enough on every hedge.

(The Prince and Westmoreland enter)

Prince Henry: How now, blown Jack! How now, quilt!

Falstaff: What, Hal! How now, mad wag! What a devil dost thou in Warwickshire?

My good Lord of Westmoreland, I cry you mercy.

I thought your honour had already been at Shrewsbury.

Earl of Westmoreland: Faith, Sir John, it is more than time that I were there, and you too; but my powers are there already.

The king, I can tell you, looks for us all: we must away all night.

Falstaff: Tut, never fear me: I am as vigilant as a cat to steal cream.

Prince Henry: I think to steal cream indeed, for thy theft hath already made thee butter, but tell me Jack, whose fellows are these that come after?

Falstaff: Mine, Hal, mine.

Prince Henry: I did never see such pitiful rascals.

Falstaff: Tut, tut, good enough to toss, food for powder, food for powder; they'll fill a pit as well as better, tush man, mortal men, mortal men.

Earl of Westmoreland: Ay, but Sir John, methinks they are exceeding poor and bare, too beggarly.

Falstaff: In faith, for their poverty, I know not where they had that, and for their bareness, I am sure they never learned that of me.

Prince Henry: No I'll be sworn unless you call three fingers on the ribs bare, but, sirrah, make haste.

Percy is already in the field.

Falstaff: What, is the king encamped?

Earl of Westmoreland: He is, Sir John, I fear we shall stay too long.

Falstaff: Well,

To the latter end of a fray and the beginning of a feast fits a dull fighter and a keen guest.

(Exeunt)

Act IV, Scene 3

The rebel camp near Shrewsbury.

(Hotspur, Worcester, Douglas, and Veron enter)

Hotspur (Henry Percy): We'll fight with him to-night.

Earl of Worcester: It may not be.

Earl of Douglas: You give him then the advantage.

Vernon: Not a whit.

Hotspur (Henry Percy): Why say you so? Looks he not for supply?

Vernon: So do we.

Hotspur (Henry Percy): His is certain, ours is doubtful.

Earl of Worcester: Good cousin, be advised; stir not tonight.

Vernon: Do not, my lord.

Earl of Douglas: You do not counsel well.

You speak it out of fear and cold heart.

Vernon: Do me no slander, Douglas: by my life, and I dare well maintain it with my life,

If well-respected honour bid me on, I hold as little counsel with weak fear as you, my lord, or any Scot that this day lives.

Let it be seen to-morrow in the battle which of us fears.

Earl of Douglas: Yea, or to-night.

Vernon: Content.

Hotspur (Henry Percy): To-night, say I.

Vernon: Come, come it may not be.

I wonder much, being men of such great leading as you are, that you foresee not what impediments drag back our expedition.

Certain horse of my cousin Vernon's are not yet come up.

Your uncle Worcester's horse came but today, and now their pride and mettle is asleep, their courage with hard labour tame and dull, that not a horse is half the half of himself.

Hotspur (Henry Percy): So are the horses of the enemy in general, journey-bated and brought low.

The better part of ours are full of rest.

Earl of Worcester: The number of the king exceedeth ours.

For God's sake, cousin, stay till all come in.

(The trumpet sounds a parley)

(Sir Walter Blunt enter)

Blunt: I come with gracious offers from the king, if you vouchsafe me hearing and respect.

Hotspur (Henry Percy): Welcome, Sir Walter Blunt; and would to God you were of our determination!

Some of us love you well, and even those some envy your great deservings and good name, because you are not of our quality, but stand against us like an enemy.

Blunt: And God defend but still I should stand so, so long as out of limit and true rule you stand against anointed majesty.

But to my charge, the king hath sent to know the nature of your griefs, and whereupon you conjure from the breast of civil peace, such bold hostility, teaching his duteous land audacious cruelty.

If that the king have any way your good deserts forgot, which he confesseth to be manifold, he bids you name your griefs; and with all speed you shall have your desires with interest and pardon absolute for yourself and these herein misled by your suggestion.

Hotspur (Henry Percy): The king is kind; and well we know the king knows at what time to promise, when to pay.

My father and my uncle and myself did give him that same royalty he wears, and when he was not six and twenty strong, sick in the world's regard, wretched and low.

A poor unminded outlaw sneaking home, my father gave him welcome to the shore and when he heard him swear and vow to God.

He came but to be Duke of Lancaster, to sue his livery and beg his peace with tears of innocency and terms of zeal.

My father, in kind heart and pity moved, swore him assistance and performed it too.

Now when the lords and barons of the realm perceived Northumberland did lean to him, the more and less came in with cap and knee; met him in boroughs, cities, villages, attended him on bridges, stood in lanes, laid gifts before him, proffered him their oaths, gave him their heirs, as pages followed him, even at the heels in golden multitudes.

He presently, as greatness knows itself, steps me a little higher than his vow made to my father, while his blood was poor, upon the naked shore at Ravenspurgh, and now, forsooth, takes on him to reform aome certain edicts and some strait decrees that lie too heavy on the commonwealth.

Cries out upon abuses, seems to weep over his country's wrongs; and by this face, this seeming brow of justice, did he win the hearts of all that he did angle for proceeded further; cut me off the heads of all the favourites that the absent king in deputation left behind him here when he was personal in the Irish war.

Blunt: Tut, I came not to hear this.

Hotspur (Henry Percy): Then to the point.

In short time after he deposed the king, soon after that deprived him of his life,and in the neck of that tasked the whole state.

To make that worse, suffered his kinsman March, who is, if every owner were well placed, indeed his king, to be engaged in Wales, there without ransom to lie forfeited; disgraced me in my happy victories sought to entrap me by intelligence.

Rated mine uncle from the council-board in rage dismissed my father from the court, broke oath on oath, committed wrong on wrong and in conclusion drove us to seek out this head of safety; and withal to pry into his title, the which we find too indirect for long continuance.

Blunt: Shall I return this answer to the king?

Hotspur (Henry Percy): Not so, Sir Walter, we'll withdraw awhile.

Go to the king and let there be impawned, some surety for a safe return again, and in the morning early shall my uncle bring him our purposes; and so farewell.

Blunt: I would you would accept of grace and love.

Hotspur (Henry Percy): And may be so we shall.

Blunt: Pray God you do.

(Exeunt)

Act IV, Scene 4

The Archbishop's palace. **(York)**

(The Archbishop and Sir Michael enter)

Archbishop Scroop: Quicken good Sir Michael, bear this sealed brief with winged haste to the lord marshal; this to my cousin Scroop, and all the rest to whom they are directed.

If you knew how much they do to import, you would make haste.

Sir Michael: My good lord, I guess their tenor.

Archbishop Scroop: Like enough you do.

To-morrow, good Sir Michael, is a day wherein the fortune of ten thousand men must bide the touch, for sir, at Shrewsbury; as I am truly given to understand the king with mighty and quick-raised power meets with Lord Harry.

And I fear, Sir Michael, what with the sickness of Northumberland, whose power was in the first proportion, and what with Owen Glendower's absence thence, who with them was a rated sinew too, and comes not in, o'er-ruled by prophecies; I fear the power of Percy is too weak to wage an instant trial with the king.

Sir Michael: Why, my good lord, you need not fear, there is Douglas and Lord Mortimer.

Archbishop Scroop: No, Mortimer is not there.

Sir Michael: But there is Mordake, Vernon, Lord Harry Percy, and there is my Lord of Worcester and a head of gallant warriors, noble gentlemen.

Archbishop Scroop: And so there is: but yet the king hath drawn the special head of all the land together.

The Prince of Wales, Lord John of Lancaster, the noble Westmoreland and warlike Blunt; and more corrivals and dear men of estimation and command in arms.

Sir Michael: Doubt not, my lord, they shall be well opposed.

Archbishop Scroop: I hope no less, yet needful it is to fear, and to prevent the worst, Sir Michael, God speed.

For if Lord Percy thrive not, were the king dismiss his power, he means to visit us, for he hath heard of our confederacy, and it is but wisdom to make strong against him; therefore make haste. I must go write again to other friends; and so farewell, Sir Michael.

(Exeunt)

Act V, Scene 1

King Henry IV's camp near Shrewsbury.

(King Henry, Prince Henry, Lord John of Lancaster, Earl of Westmoreland, Sir Walter Blunt, and Falstaff enter)

Henry IV: How bloodily the sun begins to peer above yon busky hill!

The day looks pale at his distemperature.

Prince Henry: The southern wind doth play the trumpet to his purposes, and by his hollow whistling in the leaves foretells a tempest and a blustering day.

Henry IV: Then with the losers let it sympathize, for nothing can seem foul to those that win.

(The trumpet sounds)

(Worcester and Vernon enter)

How now, my Lord of Worcester! It is not well that you and I should meet upon such terms as now we meet.

You have deceived our trust, and made us doff our easy robes of peace to crush our old limbs in ungentle steel.

This is not well, my lord, this is not well.

What say you to it? Will you again unknit this curlish knot of all-abhorred war?

And move in that obedient orb again where you did give a fair and natural light, and be no more an exhaled meteor, a prodigy of fear and a portent of broached mischief to the unborn times?

Earl of Worcester: Hear me, my liege.

For mine own part, I could be well content to entertain the lag-end of my life with quiet hours, for I do protest; I have not sought the day of this dislike.

Henry IV: You have not sought it! How comes it, then?

Falstaff: Rebellion lay in his way, and he found it.

Prince Henry: Peace, chewet, peace!

Earl of Worcester: It pleased your majesty to turn your looks of favour from myself and all our house, and yet I must remember you, my lord; we were the first and dearest of your friends.

For you my staff of office did I break in Richard's time, posted day and night to meet you on the way, and kiss your hand when yet you were in place and in account nothing so strong and fortunate as I.

It was myself, my brother and his son that brought you home and boldly did outdare the dangers of the time.

You swore to us, and you did swear that oath at Doncaster, that you did nothing purpose against the state, nor claim no further than your new-fallen right, the seat of Gaunt, dukedom of Lancaster.

To this we swore our aid, but in short space it rained down fortune showering on your head, and such a flood of greatness fell on you, what with our help, what with the absent king, what with the injuries of a wanton time.

The seeming sufferances that you had borne, and the contrarious winds that held the king so long in his unlucky Irish wars that all in England did repute him dead.

From this swarm of fair advantages you took occasion to be quickly woo'd to gripe the general sway into your hand, forget your oath to us at Doncaster; and being fed by us you used us so as that ungentle hull.

The cuckoo's bird useth the sparrow, did oppress our nest, grew by our feeding to so great a bulk that even our love durst not come near your sight for fear of swallowing; but with nimble wing we were enforced, for safety sake, to fly out of sight and raise this present head; whereby we stand opposed by such means as you yourself have forged against yourself by unkind usage, dangerous countenance and violation of all faith and troth sworn to us in your younger enterprise.

Henry IV: These things indeed you have articulate, proclaimed at market-crosses, read in churches to face the garment of rebellion with some fine colour that may please the eye of fickle changelings and poor discontents, which gape and rub the elbow at the news of hurlyburly innovation.

Never yet did insurrection want such water-colours to impaint his cause; nor moody beggars, starving for a time of pellmell havoc and confusion.

Prince Henry: In both your armies there is many a soul shall pay full dearly for this encounter, if once they join in trial

Tell your nephew, the Prince of Wales doth join with all the world in praise of Henry Percy; by my hopes this present enterprise set off his head, I do not think a braver gentleman more active-valiant or more valiant-young, more daring or more bold, is now alive to grace this latter age with noble deeds.

For my part, I may speak it to my shame, I have a truant been to chivalry; and so I hear he doth account me too.

Yet this before my father's majesty…

I am content that he shall take the odds of his great name and estimation, and will, to save the blood on either side, try fortune with him in a single fight.

Henry IV: Prince of Wales, so dare we venture thee Albeit considerations infinite, do make against it.

No, good Worcester, no, we love our people well; even those we love that are misled upon your cousin's part.

Will they take the offer of our grace, both he and they and you, every man shall be my friend again and I'll be his.

So tell your cousin, and bring me word

What he will do, but if he will not yield, rebuke and dread correction wait on us znd they shall do their office.

So, be gone, we will not now be troubled with reply; we offer fair, take it advisedly.

(Exeunt Worcester and Vernon)

Prince Henry: It will not be accepted, on my life, the Douglas and the Hotspur both together are confident against the world in arms.

Henry IV: Hence, therefore, every leader to his charge, for on their answer will we set on them; and God befriend us, as our cause is just!

(Exeunt all but Prince Henry and Falstaff)

Falstaff: Hal, if thou see me down in the battle and bestride me, so it is a point of friendship.

Prince Henry: Nothing but a colossus can do thee that friendship.

Say thy prayers, and farewell.

Falstaff: I would it were bed-time, Hal, and all well.

Prince Henry: Why, thou owest God a death.

(Prince Henry exits)

Falstaff: 'It is not due yet, I would be loath to pay him before his day.

What need I be so forward with him that calls not on me?

Well, it is no matter; honour pricks me on.

Yea, but how if honour prick me off when I come on? How then?

Can honour set to a leg? No, or an arm? No, or take away the grief of a wound? No.

Honour hath no skill in surgery then? No.

What is honour? A word. What is in that word honour? What is that honour? Air.

A trim reckoning! Who hath it? He that died on Wednesday.

Doth he feel it? No. Doth he hear it? No. It insensible then.

Yea, to the dead, but will it not live with the living? No.

Why? Detraction will not suffer it, therefore I'll none of it.

Honour is a mere scutcheon, and so ends my catechism.

(Exits)

Act V, Scene 2

The rebel camp.

(Worcester and Vernon enter)

Earl of Worcester: Oh no, my nephew must not know Sir Richard, the liberal and kind offer of the king.

Vernon: It were best he did.

Earl of Worcester: Then are we all undone.

It is not possible, it cannot be, the king should keep his word in loving us; he will suspect us still and find a time to punish this offence in other faults.

Suspicion all our lives shall be stuck full of eyes for treason is but trusted like the fox, who never so tame so cherished and locked up, will have a wild trick of his ancestors.

Look how we can, or sad or merrily, interpretation will misquote our looks, and we shall feed like oxen at a stall, the better cherished, still the nearer death.

My nephew's trespass may be well forgot, it hath the excuse of youth and heat of blood, and an adopted name of privilege; a hair-brained Hotspur, governed by a spleen.

All his offences live upon my head and on his father's, we did train him on, and his corruption being taken from us; we as the spring of all, shall pay for all; therefore good cousin, let not Harry know, in any case, the offer of the king.

Vernon: Deliver what you will, I'll say it is so.

Here comes your cousin.

(Hotspur and Douglas enter)

Hotspur (Henry Percy): My uncle is returned.

Deliver up my Lord of Westmoreland.

Uncle, what news?

Earl of Worcester: The king will bid you battle presently.

Earl of Douglas: Defy him by the Lord of Westmoreland.

Hotspur (Henry Percy): Lord Douglas, go you and tell him so.

Earl of Douglas: Merrily, and shall, and very willingly.

(Exits)

Earl of Worcester: There is no seeming mercy in the king.

Hotspur (Henry Percy): Did you beg any? God forbid!

Earl of Worcester: I told him gently of our grievances, of his oath-breaking; which he mended thus, by now forswearing that he is forsworn.

He calls us rebels, traitors; and will scourge with haughty arms this hateful name in us.

(The Earl of Douglas re-enter)

Earl of Douglas: Arm, gentlemen; to arms! For I have thrown a brave defiance in King Henry's teeth, and Westmoreland that was engaged, did bear it; which cannot choose but bring him quickly on.

Earl of Worcester: The Prince of Wales stepped forth before the king, and, nephew, challenged you to single fight.

Hotspur (Henry Percy): Oh would the quarrel lay upon our heads, and that no man might draw short breath today, but I and Harry Monmouth!

Tell me, tell me, how showed his tasking? Seemed it in contempt?

Vernon: No, by my soul; I never in my life did hear a challenge urged more modestly, unless a brother should a brother dare to gentle exercise and proof of arms.

He gave you all the duties of a man, trimmed up your praises with a princely tongue, spoke to your deservings like a chronicle, making you ever better than his praise by still dispraising praise valued in you; and which became him like a prince indeed, he made a blushing cital of himself and chid his truant youth with such a grace as if he mastered there a double spirit.

Of teaching and of learning instantly, there did he pause, but let me tell the world; if he outlive the envy of this day England did never owe so sweet a hope, so much misconstrued in his wantonness.

Hotspur (Henry Percy): Cousin, I think thou art enamoured on his follies: never did I hear of any prince so wild a libertine, but be he as he will, yet once here night I will embrace him with a soldier's arm that he shall shrink under my courtesy.

Arm, arm with speed, and, fellows, soldiers, friends better consider what you have to do than I; that have not well the gift of tongue, can lift your blood up with persuasion.

(A Messenger enters)

Messenger: My lord, here are letters for you.

Hotspur (Henry Percy): I cannot read them now. Oh gentlemen, the time of life is short!

To spend that shortness basely were too long, if life did ride upon a dial's point, still ending at the arrival of an hour; and if we live, we live to tread on kings, if die then a brave death, when princes die with us!

Now, for our consciences, the arms are fair, when the intent of bearing them is just.

(Another Messenger enters)

Messenger: My lord, prepare; the king comes on apace.

Hotspur (Henry Percy): I thank him, that he cuts me from my tale, for I profess not talking; only this, let each man do his best: and here draw I a sword, whose temper I intend to stain with the best blood that I can meet withal in the adventure of this perilous day.

Now, Esperance! Percy! And so on; sound all the lofty instruments of war, and by that music let us all embrace, for heaven to earth, some of us never shall a second time do such a courtesy.

(The trumpets sound)

(They embrace, and exeunt)

Act V, Scene 3

Plain between the camps.

(King Henry enters with his power.

Alarm: to the battle)

(Douglas and Sir Walter Blunt enter)

Blunt: What is thy name, that in the battle thus thou crossest me?

What honour dost thou seek upon my head?

Earl of Douglas: Know then, my name is Douglas, and I do haunt thee in the battle thus because some tell me that thou art a king.

Blunt: They tell thee true.

Earl of Douglas: The Lord of Stafford dear to-day hath bought thy likeness, for instead of thee, King Harry, this sword hath ended him: so shall it thee, unless thou yield thee as my prisoner.

Blunt: I was not born a yielder, thou proud Scot, and thou shalt find a king that will revenge Lord Stafford's death.

(They fight)

(Douglas kills Sir Walter Blunt)

(Hotspur enters)

Hotspur (Henry Percy): Oh Douglas, hadst thou fought at Holmedon thus, never had triumphed upon a Scot.

Earl of Douglas: All's done, all's won; here breathless lies the king.

Hotspur (Henry Percy): Where?

Earl of Douglas: Here.

Hotspur (Henry Percy): This, Douglas? No.

I know this face full well, a gallant knight he was, his name was Blunt; Semblably furnished like the king himself.

Earl of Douglas: A fool go with thy soul, whither it goes!

A borrowed title hast thou bought too dear; why didst thou tell me that thou wert a king?

Hotspur (Henry Percy): The king hath many marching in his coats.

Earl of Douglas: Now, by my sword, I will kill all his coats, I'll murder all his wardrobe, piece by piece,

Until I meet the king.

Hotspur (Henry Percy): Up, and away! Our soldiers stand full fairly for the day.

(Exeunt)

(Alarum)

(Falstaff enters solace)

Falstaff: Though I could escape shot-free at London, I fear the shot here; here's no scoring but upon the pate.

Soft! Who are you?

Sir Walter Blunt: there's honour for you! Here's no vanity!

I am as hot as moulten lead, and as heavy too.

God keep lead out of me! I need no more weight than mine own bowels.

I have led my ragamuffins where they are peppered.

There's not three of my hundred and fifty left alive, and they are for the town's end, to beg during life.

But who comes here?

(Prince Henry enters)

Prince Henry: What, stand'st thou idle here? Lend me thy sword.

Many a nobleman lies stark and stiff under the hoofs of vaunting enemies, whose deaths are yet unrevenged.

I pray to thee, lend me thy sword.

Falstaff: Oh Hal, I pray to thee, give me leave to breathe awhile.

Turk Gregory never did such deeds in arms as I have done this day.

I have paid Percy, I have made him sure.

Prince Henry: He is, indeed; and living to kill thee.

I pray to thee, lend me thy sword.

Falstaff: Nay, before God, Hal, if Percy be alive, thou get'st not my sword; but take my pistol, if thou wilt.

Prince Henry: Give it to me: what, is it in the case?

Falstaff: Ay Hal, it is hot, it is hot; there's that will sack a city.

(Prince Henry draws it out, and finds it to be a bottle of sack)

Prince Henry: What, is it a time to jest and dally now?

(He throws the bottle at him)

(Exits)

Falstaff: Well, if Percy be alive, I'll pierce him.

If he do come in my way, so: if he do not, if I come in his willingly, let him make a carbonado of me.

I like not such grinning honour as Sir Walter hath, give me life; which if I can save, so, if not honour comes unlooked for, and there's an end.

(Falstaff exits)

Act V, Scene 4

Another part of the field.

(Alarm)

(Prince Henry, Lord John of Lancaster, and Earl of Westmoreland enter)

Prince Henry: I pray to thee, hurry, withdraw thyself; thou bleed'st too much.

Lord John of Lancaster, go you with him.

Prince John: Not I, my lord, unless I did bleed too.

I beseech your majesty, make up, lest your retirement do amaze your friends.

Prince Henry: I will do so, My Lord of Westmoreland, lead him to his tent.

Earl of Westmoreland: Come, my lord, I'll lead you to your tent.

Prince Henry: Lead me, my lord? I do not need your help, and God forbid a shallow scratch should drive the Prince of Wales from such a field as this; where stained nobility lies trodden on and rebels' arms triumph in massacres!

Prince John: We breathe too long: come, cousin Westmoreland, our duty this way lies; for God's sake come.

(Exeunt Lancaster and Westmoreland)

Prince Henry: By God, thou hast deceived me, Lancaster; I did not think thee lord of such a spirit before, I loved thee as a brother John, but now I do respect thee as my soul.

Prince Henry: I saw him hold Lord Percy at the point with lustier maintenance than I did look for of such an ungrown warrior.

Prince Henry: Oh this boy lends metal to us all!

(Exit)

(Enter Douglas)

Earl of Douglas: Another king! they grow like Hydra's heads:

I am the Douglas, fatal to all those

That wear those colours on them: what art thou, 2980

That counterfeit'st the person of a king?

Henry IV: The king himself; who, Douglas, grieves at heart

So many of his shadows thou hast met

And not the very king. I have two boys

Seek Percy and thyself about the field: 2985

But, seeing thou fall'st on me so luckily,

I will assay thee: so, defend thyself.

Earl of Douglas: I fear thou art another counterfeit;

And yet, in faith, thou bear'st thee like a king:

But mine I am sure thou art, whoe'er thou be, 2990

And thus I win thee.

(They fight. King Henry being in danger, Prince Henry enters)

Prince Henry: Hold up thy head, vile Scot, or thou art like

Never to hold it up again! the spirits

Of valiant Shirley, Stafford, Blunt, are in my arms: 2995

It is the Prince of Wales that threatens thee;

Who never promiseth but he means to pay.

(They fight)

(Douglas flies)

Cheerly, my lord. how fares your grace?

Sir Nicholas Gawsey hath for succor sent, 3000

And so hath Clifton: I'll to Clifton straight.

Prince Henry: Stay, and breathe awhile:

Thou hast redeem'd thy lost opinion,

And show'd thou makest some tender of my life,

In this fair rescue thou hast brought to me.

Prince Henry: Oh God! they did me too much injury

That ever said I hearken'd for your death.

If it were so, I might have let alone

The insulting hand of Douglas over you,

Which would have been as speedy in your end 3010

As all the poisonous potions in the world

And saved the treacherous labour of your son.

Prince Henry: Make up to Clifton: I'll to Sir Nicholas Gawsey.

(Exit)

(Hotspur enters)

Hotspur (Henry Percy): If I mistake not, thou art Harry Monmouth.

Prince Henry: Thou speak'st as if I would deny my name.

Hotspur (Henry Percy): My name is Harry Percy.

Prince Henry: Why, then I see

A very valiant rebel of the name. I am the Prince of Wales; and think not, Percy, to share with me in glory any more.

Two stars keep not their motion in one sphere, nor can one England brook a double reign, of Harry Percy and the Prince of Wales.

Hotspur (Henry Percy): Nor shall it, Harry; for the hour is come

To end the one of us; and would to God

Thy name in arms were now as great as mine!

Prince Henry: I'll make it greater ere I part from thee and all the budding honours on thy crest; I'll crop to make a garland for my head.

Hotspur (Henry Percy): I can no longer brook thy vanities.

(They fight)

(Falstaff enters)

Falstaff: Well said, Hal! To it Hal! Nay, you shall find no boy's play here, I can tell you.

(Douglas re-enters; he fights with Falstaff who falls down as if he were dead, and exit Douglas, Hotspur is wounded, and falls)

Hotspur (Henry Percy): Oh Harry, thou hast robb'd me of my youth!

I better brook the loss of brittle life than those proud titles thou hast won of me, they wound my thoughts worse than sword my flesh, but thought's the slave of life, and life time's fool; and time that takes survey of all the world must have a stop.

Oh I could prophesy, but that the earthy and cold hand of death lies on my tongue: no, Percy, thou art dust and food for.

(Dies)

Prince Henry: For worms, brave Percy: fare thee well, great heart!

Ill-weaved ambition, how much art thou shrunk!

When that this body did contain a spirit, a kingdom for it was too small a bound; but now two paces of the vilest earth is room enough.

This earth that bears thee dead bears not alive so stout a gentleman.

If thou wert sensible of courtesy, I should not make so dear a show of zeal, but let my favours hide thy mangled face; and even in thy behalf I'll thank myself for doing these fair rites of tenderness.

Adieu, and take thy praise with thee to heaven!

Thy ignominy sleep with thee in the grave, but not remember'd in thy epitaph!

(He spieth Falstaff on the ground)

What, old acquaintance! Could not all this flesh keep in a little life?

Poor Jack, farewell! I could have better spared a better man.

Oh I should have a heavy miss of thee, if I were much in love with vanity!

Death hath not struck so fat a deer to-day, though many dearer, in this bloody fray embowelled; will I see thee by and by, till then in blood by noble Percy lie.

(Prince Henry exits)

Falstaff: (Rising up) Embowelled! if thou embowel me to-day, I'll give you leave to powder me and eat me too to-morrow.

It is blood, it was time to counterfeit, or that hot termagant Scot had paid me scot and lot too.

Counterfeit? I lie, I am no counterfeit, to die is to be a counterfeit; for he is but the counterfeit of a man who hath not the life of a man, but to counterfeit dying, when a man thereby liveth is to be no counterfeit, but the true and perfect image of life indeed.

The better part of valour is discretion in the which better part I have saved mylife.

I am afraid of this gunpowder Percy, though he be dead; how if he should counterfeit too and rise? By my faith I am afraid he would prove the better counterfeit, therefore I'll make him sure, yea, and I'll swear I killed him.

Why may not he rise as well as I? Nothing confutes me but eyes, and nobody sees me, therefore, sirrah.

(Stabbing him)

With a new wound in your thigh, come you along with me.

(Takes up Hotspur on his back)

(Prince Henry and Lord John of Lancaster re-enter)

Prince Henry: Come, brother John, full bravely hast thou fleshed thy maiden sword.

Prince John: But, soft! Whom have we here?

Did you not tell me this fat man was dead?

Prince Henry: I did; I saw him dead, breathless and bleeding on the ground.

Art thou alive? Or is it fantasy that plays upon our eyesight?

I pray to thee, speak, we will not trust our eyes without our ears: thou art not what thou seem'st.

Falstaff: No, that's certain, I am not a double man; but if I be not Jack Falstaff, then am I a Jack.

There is Percy.

(Throwing the body down)

If your father will do me any honour, so, if not, let him kill the next Percy himself.

I look to be either earl or duke, I can assure you.

Prince Henry: Why, Percy I killed myself and saw thee dead.

Falstaff: Didst thou? Lord, Lord, how this world is given to lying!

I grant you I was down and out of breath, and so was he: but we rose both at an instant and fought a long hour by Shrewsbury clock.

If I may be believed, so if not, let them that should reward valour bear the sin upon their own heads.

I'll take it upon my death, I gave him this wound in the thigh.

If the man were alive and would deny it, I would make him eat a piece of my sword.

Prince John: This is the strangest tale that ever I heard.

Prince Henry: This is the strangest fellow, brother John.

Come, bring your luggage nobly on your back; for my part, if a lie may do thee grace, I'll gild it with the happiest terms I have.

(A retreat is sounded)

The trumpet sounds retreat; the day is ours.

Come, brother, let us to the highest of the field to see what friends are living, who are dead.

(Exeunt Prince Henry and Lancaster)

Falstaff: I'll follow, as they say, for reward.

He that rewards me, God reward him!

If I do grow great, I'll grow less, for I'll purge and leave sack, and live cleanly as a nobleman should do.

(Exits)

Act V, Scene 5

Another part of the field.

(The trumpets sounds)

(King Henry IV, Prince Henry, Lord John Lancaster, EARL OF Westmoreland enter with Worcester, and Vernon with prisoners)

Henry IV: Thus ever did rebellion find rebuke.

Ill-spirited Worcester! did not we send grace, pardon and terms of love to all of you?

Wouldst thou turn our offers contrary? Misuse the tenor of thy kinsman's trust?

Three knights upon our party slain to-day, a noble earl and many a creature else had been alive this hour, if like a Christian thou hadst truly borne between our armies true intelligence.

Earl of Worcester: What I have done my safety urged me to, and I embrace this fortune patiently, since not to be avoided it falls on me.

Henry IV: Bear Worcester to the death and Vernon too; other offenders we will pause upon.

(Exeunt Worcester and Vernon, guarded)

How goes the field?

Prince Henry: The noble Scot, Lord Douglas, when he saw the fortune of the day quite turned from him; the noble Percy slain, and all his men upon the foot of fear, fled with the rest falling from a hill, he was so bruised that the pursuers took him.

At my tent the Douglas is, and I beseech your grace I may dispose of him.

Henry IV: With all my heart.

Prince Henry: Then, brother John of Lancaster, to you this honourable bounty shall belong: go to the Douglas, and deliver him up to his pleasure, ransomless and free.

His valour shown upon our crests to-day hath taught us how to cherish such high deeds even in the bosom of our adversaries.

Prince John: I thank your grace for this high courtesy, which I shall give away immediately.

Henry IV: Then this remains, that we divide our power.

You, son John, and my cousin Westmoreland towards York shall bend you with your dearest speedtTo meet Northumberland and the prelate Scroop; who as we hear, are busily in arms, myself and you, son Harry, will towards Wales, to fight with Glendower and the Earl of March.

Rebellion in this land shall lose his sway, meeting the cheque of such another day, and since this business so fair is done, let us not leave till all our own be won.

(Exeunt)

The End

Description of Titles

The Comedy of Errors
Caught in a land of embittered woman and war, caught in months of strife, where a merchant's visit offers little natural relief. The fleeting moment of approving gold, inspire further bitterness, upon an approach to the marketplace, and then the women that occupy within them.

19 Characters

The Taming of the Shrew
Arrangements are made to spencer would be suiters to melt the splendors of a strong willed women. The winning is found pledged, influencing maids to seek their turns, and meanwhile terms required, an authentic spirit that they will/would wed soon.

34 Characters

Love's Labor's Lost
The house of a scholarly pursuit, returns into an expressive, either poetic or drunken as highlighting the gold-slur filled house of charms and dance like rhymes

19 Characters

A Midsummer Night's Dream
Journey into a land of fairies, where creatures are found to have the same issues as nobilities. Exemplifying, perhaps, there's no place like home. Meet fairies as they frolic and play the noble hearts and sway, posed in the recesses of night, and mystic lands of a faraway kingdom.

22 Characters

The Merchant of Venice

An angry Shylock brings to trial a merchant, over a lover's quarrel disrupted, demanding pounds of flesh. With no desires for even three times the amount, the Shylock demands his vengeance at heart.

22 Characters

The Merry Wives of Windsor
Mistresses and lords try and relate towards one another, as various important community figures come to have their word/seek the hostesses. Pleasantries are exchanged as a range of charms are expressed, until conversation resembled so to folly.

23 Characters

Much Ado About Nothing
Soldiery level consideration occupy the gossip, as several hostilities are summoned up, onto heart related matter. Also in conflict. The latter portion of the story lightens up to a women's home and pleasantries. Thereafter, a general search and care in actions, creating response phrasing poetic to the responses of leadership parading, until an end full of sensitivity asking gently questions, onto kisses

23 Characters

As You Like It
Troubled lower nobles venture about daily business, with some mild graces towards the ladies found. In need of relief or play, the Duke and family members take to the woods, where jests of drinking turn into troubled amusements, or warmth of a women's heart.

26 Characters

Troilus and Cressida
The infamous Greek battle for Troy. A large army arrives to take back the lost love of a humiliated foe. Both sides mobilize heroes onto the field, as soldiers and generals move to the side, and let strategies and fate take their course.

21+ Characters

All's Well That Ends Well
A tale of delightful, womanly gossip of a prestigious sort, until the French King has his word on the excellence of others. The story initially revolves around a strong willed countess, whose courteous pose and insight, reflect a nobility reflective of the house and court (council). Dialogue therein revolving around the councils rather, to exemplify (court counselling women).

25 Characters

Measure for Measure
Statesmen discourse leading with time to a personal reflection. Strolling Dukes and strong willed women occupy the background, where high-function status and family discourse intertwine within formalities (of administrative foresight, expression) observed.

24 Characters

Richard III
An in palace drama with King Richard the 3rd, Queen Elizabeth, and Queen Margret. Onto a haunting reunion, as the state processes royal executions.

61+ Characters

The Life and Death of King John
King John and Queen Elinor entertain the royal court, where a bastard has come to make his day. Strategic deployments of influence are exemplified, as the bastard plots about until alerts, alarm corruption has delivered trouble makers known.

24 Characters

Romeo and Juliet
Lovers emerge within a city gripped with two feuding houses apposed. As turmoil are caught in bitter heat, the lover's. Bliss and undying pledge becomes them, onto the eternal soul (of love and romance).

33 Characters

Othello
A hopeful Othello calls upon the favor of allies based on proposed merits, which called upon allies and foes to him. In a mixed response, allies and foes campaign both against Othello, becoming a bitter, personal tangle over a mislead love adventure representing the future of either fates

25 Characters

Macbeth
A desperate Macbeth ventures towards witches to tell fortune, returning to a castle haunted by ghost/old-spirits. Macbeth's worries become frightful nightmares, along the despair of the household around him.

39 Characters

Mark Antony and Cleopatra

The relations or affections of Mark Anthony and Cleopatra, onto the strategic interactions between Mark Anthony and Octavius. The discourse moves to the Octavius house, revealing Octavia, and later then, Pompey in the background. Overall the focus retains upon Mark Anthony, Cleopatra, and Octavius.

56+ Characters

Coriolanus

Citizens riot during a famine, while the state administrative intervenes and otherwise discourses the seriousness of the matter and war. Lady's calm the general ambience, until the sword is mobilized to defend the gates, , while the plight of people is nevertheless heard convincing Roman elites the problem is being found/fought within.

60 Characters

Pericles Prince of Tyre

A thoughtful/reflective Pericles interposes his good will and well-meaning nature, which leads him to visit fishermen friends, and onto state function. Pericles is then confronted, required to (take a plunge) to marry, embedding him deeper into ocean stock of sea life among sailors experience and merchant owners, investing his interest as babe, securing his destiny as then, future king

44 Characters

Cymbeline

Cymbeline, friend or loyalist to the first Caesars, is summoned into battle. Meanwhile there are personal matters to attend to within the noble house.

41 Characters

The Winter's Tale
A gossipy tale of high office, administrative daily insight onto the tender meaning of things and people an how they unite unwittingly at the discourse of their respected hierarchies of partnership. Profoundness therein inspiring the recounts of clown and child, as examples perhaps of what state administration and or nobility's company keeps.

34+ Characters

The Tempest
After an earth shattering storm, a fairy dwelling world is found. There magic and graces are there in song, glory and praises.

21 Characters

The Two Gentlemen of Verona
Loving beginnings, yet far too. General virtues going upwards in hierarchies, with overall chivalrous wits.

Twelfth Night
An evening in the company of sound gatherings, seemingly a docile manner recount version of noble delights. In similarities of the pose, composing an environment of insight and oversight.

Henry the 8th
Across chamber and palace, Dukes and lords, until Queen Katharine's and King Henry VIII's present their graces, conversing the Cardinal then. The signs then, an Elizabeth is born.

Richard II
King Richard the 2nd readies the armed forces at the sound of alarm, while later Henry IV is near for discussion. King Richard the 2nd and his groom.

Henry V
King Henry the 5th, as found across his palace, until a readiness for war. King Henry the 5th and the French King, with armies both have at it.

Henry VI, Part 1
Funeral of King Henry the 5th, Henry VI makes his approach to France. Henry VI fashions as thy lord protector.

Henry VI, Part 2
King Henry the 6th, where the Cardinal is seen mocking protectors with praise, as all the rage. Queen Margaret at King Henry VI, until the end.

Henry VI, Part 3
King Henry VI is busy fighting a succession of battles, France and England as having at it, yet again.

King Henry the 5th
King Henry 5 fight his way toward France, they reach the peaceful and loving responses of a French King.

Henry IV, Part 1
King Henry the 4th, from Palace to Pub, onto the battle fields again. Until there is no rebellion.

Henry IV, Part 2
Henry IV, from Palace, Priest and then tavern, he nevertheless finds some peace, after reflection. King Henry IV, and then King Henry V as fashionable by the end.

Titus Andronicus
A story of Romans and Goths, where roman sways give way. And then to see about Goths and proving worthiness.

28 Characters

Julius Caesar
Near the Final days of the 1st Caesar, and the continuation everlasting as through Octavius.

Hamlet
Hamlet, and his father the King, the father yet a Ghost. Hamlet, not so eager to join.

King Lear
King Lear, from palace to castle, to fighting the French in the field. After battle King Lear is in bed, the Doctor discourses, what lays then now, will have an impact upon the end.

Timon of Athens
A story set in Greece, a place of poets and cultured, good graces. From Arts and daily expressive, to political and charmed.

www.ingramcontent.com/pod-product-compliance
Lightning Source LLC
Chambersburg PA
CBHW051434290426
44109CB00016B/1549